TEACHER'S GUIDE

YEARS 1-2

PART B

The Q Science Teacher's Guides have been written with the aim of providing easily accessible, background information for each of the children's books.

This edition contains full reference to the National Curriculum for Science for implementation from August 1992.

For Years 1 and 2 (Key Stage 1) there are two Teacher's Guides, Part A and Part B. This Guide covers the individual explorations in Exploring Science Book 2, followed by each of the books in Science Themes *Earth, Atmosphere and Space* and *Communications.*

CONTENTS

EXPLORING SCIENCE

BOOK 2

TOPIC: ANIMAL ALLSORTS

BABY ANIMALS

• Make a scrap book to show what babies need to help them grow. Show how people change from babies to grown ups.
• What do different animals need to learn in order to survive, eg lions to hunt, birds of prey to fly and dive for prey?

ANIMALS SEASONS

• Do all animals behave in the same way all year round?

PETS

• Which animals do we keep as pets? Why? Do people in other countries keep different ones?
• Make a happy home for a pet. What do you need to think about?

ANIMALS ALLSORTS

ANIMALS OF LONG AGO

• Draw a large picture showing where animals of long ago lived. Did they all eat the same food?

DAY TO DAY LIVING

• Make a diary of what you do at different times during the day and night.
• How do animals spend their days and nights, eg pets? Nocturnal animals. Animals such as lions which only eat every few days.

HUMANS

• How are you different from other animals? How are you similar to other animals?
• Consider how humans differ (see also *Me and my friends*).

CROSS-CURRICULAR LINKS

Maths: Data handling — looking at pets within the class group and graphing results. Classifying animals into groups, eg with fur/without fur, with wings/without wings. Move on to formal classification — mammals, birds, etc. Use pictures from magazines.

History: When did the dinosaurs live? When did the dodo becomes extinct? Why? Do we keep the same pets nowadays as our grandparents used to?

Technology: Designing safe toys for pets, animals feeders, animal baths.

English: Stories involving your pet (or the pet you would like to own). Descriptions of imaginary animals you might meet if you visited another planet.
Poems
Birds, Beasts and Fishes, Anne Carter and Reg Cartwright, (Walker Books)
I saw, Story time, Rhinoceros stew, Gorilla, Cows, The butterfly, Hippopotamuses, from *Another first poetry book* compiled by John Foster (Oxford).
Stories
Panther's moon and other stories Ruskin Bond (Puffin)
The village dinosaur Phyllis Arkle (Puffin)

ANIMALS ALLSORTS

EXPLORATION: 1.	How are you different from other animals? How are you similar to other animals?

WAYS FORWARD

It would be useful for children to draw a human and label parts of it.

Ask the class to brainstorm as many animals as they can. The children could look through magazines and cut out pictures of animals. What do some animals have that others don't, eg live young, eggs, beak, number of legs, feather, gills, fur, scales, webbed feet, wings?

Children could group such animals according to what features they have, eg birds have feathers; insects have six legs; fish have gills; mammals have live young. They could also group animals according to where they live, eg underground, in the Sea, in woods/forest, in grassland. How are animals adapted to where they live? Scrapbooks and posters or charts could be made to show animal groupings. Which group does man fit into? What do animals all have in common, eg animals take in food and produce waste materials are able to move from one spot; grow bigger from child to adult; can produce others of their own kind; respond to cold/hot/light; generally breath oxygen and produce carbon dioxide. They could compare the size of animals with one another.

The children could create a database on the computer and make games based on animal features, eg Snap, Happy families, What am I?, 20 questions.

A visit to a zoo or wildlife park might be useful.

As an extension, look at how animals are adapted to their environment through camouflage. Investigate animals such as the chameleon, stoat and iguana which change colour according to their environment/season. What ideas does man use which he has gained from animals, eg wearing fake fur in winter, camouflage for soldiers? Consider also warning colours used in nature (yellow and black) and how animals mimic one another for defensive reasons.

Consider which animals are closest to us — apes, eg chimpanzees, gorillas, etc — and how they compare to us.

MATERIALS NEEDED AND SAFETY POINTS

- Magazines containing pictures of animals.
- Reference books about animals in order to help children group them.
- Large sheets of paper, crayons/felt tip pens/pencils in order to produce charts.
- Reference books about evolution.
- Any videos, films or pictures about animals in particular habitats, eg forest, pond, sea.

NATIONAL CURRICULUM ASSESSMENT OPPORTUNITIES

Sc 1 / 1a	Sc 1 / 3a	Sc 2 / 1a	Sc 2 / 3a
2a	3b	1b	
2b		2b	
2c		2c	

EXPLORATION: 2.   Do all the animals behave in the same way all year around?

WAYS FORWARD

Ask children to think about and observe animals around the school, eg birds, insects, hedgehogs, squirrels, foxes, butterflies. Do they see these animals all year round? (Children could carry out a survey over the year to see how the occurrence of these animals varies over the year.) Do childrens' pets behave the same way all year round (eg tortoises hibernate)? Do farmers carry out the same activities all year round (eg lambing season in spring)? What happens to butterflies and hedgehogs, badgers and squirrels in winter? Life cycles may be introduced, eg of frog, butterfly, moth. Children could investigate these using reference books. Migration of birds might be discussed and also nest building and egg laying in the Spring. Which birds stay in Britain and which migrate?

Children could make charts/pictograms/friezes/scrapbooks/bar charts/databases of which animals they see around school during each season.

Is the way animals behave related to the plants which are growing best/flowering during each season? For example, bees collect pollen from flowers in Summer, squirrels collect nuts in the Winter.

MATERIALS NEEDED AND SAFETY POINTS

- Paper, pencils, crayons.
- Binoculars (for observing birds and other animals from a distance).
- Reference books.
- Any charts/films/videos/referring to different seasons.
- Magnifying glasses for observing insects more closely.

NATIONAL CURRICULUM ASSESSMENT OPPORTUNITIES

Sc 1 / 1a	Sc 2 / 1b	Sc 4 / 2b
2b	2a	
2c	2b	
3a	2c	
3c	3a	
3d	3b	

ANIMALS ALLSORTS

EXPLORATION: 3. Make a happy home for a pet. What do you need to think about?

WAYS FORWARD

Encourage the children to think of the things which all animals need to live (food, warmth, oxygen, water and a place to breed).

How much water does their pet need (fish can't live outside water)? How does it move/exercise — have they given it the opportunity to do so, eg rabbit-run, hamster play things? To be happy, does it need to be let out occasionally, eg budgie, rabbit?

Could children make a pet care manual for this animal, including how often it needs time out from its home?

Humans like to keep clean; how does this pet wash? Have they given it the opportunity to do so? Is its living area large enough? Has it got somewhere to sleep and material so that it can make a bed?

What does it eat in the wild? How can a substitute be provided? Does it need treats ocasionally to be happy? If so, what? Does its home need to be waterproof? Would it be happier with a companion?

MATERIALS NEEDED AND SAFETY POINTS

- A variety of books about pets and pet care manuals. Perhaps a few toys made for animals.
- A selection of junk including large boxes and plastic bottles, dowelling, yoghurt pots, round lids, cotton reels, polythene, PVA glue. (It may be useful to have a glue gun to hand for the teacher to use for sticking some materials).
- Fabric, scrap paper.
- A useful book is *A child's guide to caring for pets*, Gerald and Julie Hawksley (Victoria House).

NATIONAL CURRICULUM ASSESSMENT OPPORTUNITIES

Sc 1 / 1a	Sc 2 / 1b
2a	2a
3a	2b
	2c
	3a

ANIMAL ALLSORTS

> **EXPLORATION: 4.** **Make a scrap book to show what babies need to help them grow. Show how people change from babies into grown-ups.**

WAYS FORWARD

Encourage children to think about babies which they know, eg brother, sister, neighbour, etc. Perhaps a parent with a baby, or a midwife could visit and talk about baby care. Look at baby catalogues — what do they feature and why, eg feeding bottles, blankets, walking toys, cot toys, bath toys, toys to encourage children to talk?

Why does the food babies eat change? Look at different types of food and consider what each does, eg carbohydrates give energy, protein helps repair and growth, calcium helps create strong teeth and bones.

Why do babies' clothes change as they grow, eg when they learn to crawl, toddle? When considering how children grow, the children could be encouraged to bring in photographs of themselves as babies and perhaps previous school photos to show how they've changed. The children might look at photos of their parents, or other relatives as children, and see how they have changed over time.

How do the children in the nursery differ from the top infants or top juniors? Do they enjoy different games, speak differently? Are older children taller, broader, stronger?

As an extension, consider the skills which other animals need to learn as they grow and develop. How are they taught and which happen automatically, eg dogs walking, birds flying, cats hunting, fish swimming? Perhaps the children could watch how animals such as a baby mouse and its mother develop in the classroom.

MATERIALS NEEDED AND SAFETY POINTS

- Baby catalogues, photos of babies (children as babies).
- Rulers, string, book-making materials, glue, coloured pencils and other materials for drawing/painting.
- Baby clothes/toys and apparatus for preparing food (if available).
- Baby care books.
- For extension work, books about baby animals.

NATIONAL CURRICULUM ASSESSMENT OPPORTUNITIES

Sc 1 / 1a	Sc 2 / 1a
2a	1b
2b	2a
	2b
	3a

ANIMALS ALLSORTS

EXPLORATION: 5.	**Draw a large picture showing where animals of long ago lived. Did they all eat the same food?**

WAYS FORWARD

This could be done as a whole class activity with the children divided into groups.

There are many animals still alive today whose species has been alive for many years, eg wolf, tortoise, horse, crocodile, rhinoceros.

Children could create a freize showing animals in different sections — in the air, above ground, below ground, in water (sea/rivers/ponds and lakes). They might also consider animals which are nearly extinct or have recently become extinct, eg great awk, or dodo. The sabre-toothed tiger and woolly mammoth could also be included.

Children in general love dinosaurs as a topic and obviously there are many different dinosaurs to consider some of which ate each other! Remember also that not all dinosaurs lived at the same time.

The children could try to draw their animals to scale. How can we stop animals from becoming extinct?

As an extension consider animals which are near to extinction now and how their extinction could be prevented, eg tiger, elephant, some whales. The passenger pigeon in North America only became extinct in the 1930s, when its population was decimated through shooting.

MATERIALS NEEDED AND SAFETY POINTS

- Large pieces of paper and drawing/painting/collage material.
- A selection of reference books about prehistoric animals.
- Conservation books and leaflets. (The World Wildlife Fund for Nature provides useful materials for children on conservation of animals.)

NATIONAL CURRICULUM ASSESSMENT OPPORTUNITIES

Sc 1 / 2a	Sc 2 / 1a
2b	2a
2c	2b
	2c
	3a

EXPLORATION: 6. Make a diary of what you do at different times during the day and night.

WAYS FORWARD

Ask the children to split their day into four time bands — morning/afternoon/evening/night — and keep a diary (in written or pictorial form) over 2 - 7 days of what they did during those time bands. For comparison, older children may include a weekend. A general class record of the school day could also be kept. Pictograms/pie charts and bar charts/databases could be produced to show activities carried out on different days.

Children might discuss which activities they carry out every day. They could consider which they do to keep alive, eg eating and which to keep healthy, eg running, sleeping, washing. Does what they do at night differ as much as what they do during the day?

Children could create different symbols for different activities in order to make recording easier.

As an extension, consider how what you do is affected by other factors, eg the weather and illness. Do we spend more/less time on certain activities according to the season?

MATERIALS NEEDED AND SAFETY POINTS

- Paper (plain and squared).
- Pencils, crayons, rulers.
- A clock on the wall if older/able children wish to record their activities over a shorter time such as an hour.

NATIONAL CURRICULUM ASSESSMENT OPPORTUNITIES

Sc 1 / 1a   Sc 2 / 3a
     2a
     2b
     3a

TOPIC: MY SCHOOL

ENVIRONMENT

- Make a collection of things that remind you of the season.
- Be safe. Be healthy. What should we do?
- Make a record of the plants and animals you see around school. What do they need to stay alive? How can we help?
- Things around your school can look old and worn because of the weather. Draw them.

BUILDINGS AND INTERIOR

- What building materials have been used around your school?
- Find out what electricity is used for in school.
Show your results.
- Make a collection of as many different materials as you can. Sort out the materials.

MY SCHOOL

PEOPLE

- Find out some interesting facts about children and grown-ups in your school.

CROSS-CURRICULAR LINKS

Technology:	Design and make a model of an ideal school.
Geography:	Simple mapping of children's routes/journeys to school, and catchment area. How far do children come? Who travels the furthest? Examination of plans of the school's interior and a bird's eye view of the school.
Art:	Sketching/painting views of the school.
English:	**Poems** From Please Mrs Butler verses by Allan Ahlberg (Puffin Books). From School's Out! compiled by John Foster (OUP).

MY SCHOOL

EXPLORATION: 1. What building materials have been used around your school?

WAYS FORWARD

Consider first the school shown in the children's book, and the different materials which have been used to build it. Can they name the materials marked with a question mark (glass for windows, bricks for the out-building, wood for the cycle shed, concrete for the pavement)?

Tour your own school with the children, examining the materials, making rubbings and collecting examples if possible.

Group buildings and objects according to what materials they are made of.   Discuss the suitability of the different materials which have been used, eg plastic for bins and drain pipes (rust proof and durable), concrete for walls (strong, water resistant), glass for windows (transparent, strong, water resistant).

Discuss how some of the materials are made, eg concrete from gravel and cement, brick from baked clay, plastic from chemicals and by-products of materials such as coal.

MATERIALS NEEDED AND SAFETY POINTS

- Paper, pencils, pens for making rubbings.
- Supervision for school tour.

NATIONAL CURRICULUM ASSESSMENT OPPORTUNITIES

Sc 1 / 1a   Sc 3 / 1
    2a   2a
                 3a

MY SCHOOL

> ### EXPLORATION: 2. Find out some interesting facts about children and grown-ups in your school.

WAYS FORWARD

Encourage children to use a variety of methods for gathering and collating facts, eg cassette tape recordings, questionnaires.

For the collation, they could physically group items, graph results by hand or use a simple computer database.

Children could find out:
- Which months people were born in.
- People's hair and eye colours.
- Which are the most common hobbies?
- Which are the most commonly kept pets?
- Which are the most commonly read newspapers?
- Favourite foods and colours.

Encourage children to predict and draw conclusions from their findings when possible, for example that dark-haired people generally have dark eyes.

MATERIALS NEEDED AND SAFETY POINTS

- Computer database, eg *Our facts*.
- Tape recorder.
- Paper and clip boards for collecting information.

NATIONAL CURRICULUM ASSESSMENT OPPORTUNITIES

Sc 1 / 1a   Sc 2 / 1b (part)
     2a
     2c
     3a

EXPLORATION : 3. Make a collection of things that remind you of the season.

WAYS FORWARD

Start by discussing each season in turn with the children, to sort out what the essential characteristics are.

What activities do the children do in different seasons? Are there any places they go to, or activities they do, more often in one or two seasons than the others, eg playing football, going to the park, the beach or the swimming pool, staying indoors and watching TV?

What is different about the clothes they wear in different seasons?

How does the view out of their classroom window change during the year?

Set up an interest table for the current season, or perhaps one for each season of the year. Ask children to bring in items, from home as well as from around the school. Identify the objects. Postcards and photographs could be included if relevant.

MATERIALS NEEDED AND SAFETY POINTS

- Remind children not to eat any items.
- Children should take care when looking for plants - ideally, they should be photographed but if any plants are picked, they must not be pulled out by the roots.

NATIONAL CURRICULUM ASSESSMENT OPPORTUNITIES

Sc 1 / 1a   Sc 2 / 1b
                      2a (part)
                      2b

MY SCHOOL

EXPLORATION : 4.   Be safe. Be healthy.   What should we do?

WAYS FORWARD

Children could examine the following safety aspects:
- The proper use of bins to prevent litter spreading. Experiment to find out which litter is biodegradable and which is not.
- Electrical safety. Consider the proper use of plugs/plug points and items using electricity, and the dangers of mis-use.
- Consideration for others in moving about school and in games at play time. What should they take care to do, eg not to run in school, keep hard footballs away from unsuspecting children not involved?
- Safety on the roads when coming to school, for example using the zebra crossing.
- The importance of knowing what to do in the case of an emergency, eg a fit.
- Safety with fireworks, eg adults should always light them, everyone should stand well back from them.
- The importance of fire precautions — fire drill, fire extinguishers and blankets.
- What to do in the event of minor accidents and injuries — first aid cabinets.

Children should examine the following health aspects:
- Wearing appropriate clothes outdoors, eg coats in cold weather.
- Selecting healthy snacks for play time, such as fruit.
- Washing hands after using the toilet.

Children could design an appropriate 'healthy and safe' poster.

MATERIALS NEEDED AND SAFETY POINTS

- Clipboards.
- Paper for children to record observations.
- Materials for designing posters.

Safety
- Children should always wear plastic gloves when handling rubbish.

NATIONAL CURRICULUM ASSESSMENT OPPORTUNITIES

Sc 1 /1a	Sc 2 / 2a	Sc 4 / 1a
	2d	3a

EXPLORATION : 5.   Make a record of the plants and animals you see around school. What do they need to stay alive? How can we help?

WAYS FORWARD

Help children to make an appropriate chart:

Names of animal/plant	Where found

Group the animals and plants, eg animals with four legs, animals with six legs, flowering plants, non-flowering plants.

Plants can also be grouped by their leaf shape.

Consider the needs of the animals and the plants in order to stay alive. Try growing some plants indoors, such as cress seeds. Consider the factors needed for successful growth — light, water, appropriate soil, temperature. Design fair tests to find out about these factors, eg placing plants in different places of varying light in the classroom, but keeping other factors (water, temperature, soil) the same. Measure the growth of the plants.

Consider man's impact on the environment — the building of a road and the pollution from the traffic can kill plants and make it difficult for animals to cross safely. We can help by looking after the animals and plants in the school.

MATERIALS NEEDED AND SAFETY POINTS

- Paper and pencils for records, or a computer for recording information.

NATIONAL CURRICULUM ASSESSMENT OPPORTUNITIES

Sc 1 / 1a	Sc 2 / 1a
2a	1b
2b	2a (part)
2c	2b
3a	3b
3b	3c
3c	
3d	

MY SCHOOL

EXPLORATION : 6. Things around your school can look old and worn because of the weather. Draw them.

WAYS FORWARD

Carry out some experiments in the classroom and discuss the results:
- What does the Sun do to materials? For example, it fades coloured paper and dries out clay, making it crack.
- What does the rain/water do? For example it causes paper to wrinkle, paint to peel, nails to rust.

Help children to search for signs of weathering around the school, eg faded paintwork, peeling paint, rusty drain pipes, cracked stone or bricks, small trees or bushes bent by the wind, maybe plants shrivelled because of lack of water.

What sort of weather do they think has mostly caused each sign of weathering?

MATERIALS NEEDED AND SAFETY POINTS

- Materials for classroom experiments, eg coloured paper, clay, nails.
- Paper and pens/pencils to draw findings.
- Perhaps a camera to photograph some findings.

NATIONAL CURRICULUM ASSESSMENT OPPORTUNITIES

Sc 1 / 1a   Sc 3 / 3c
     2a
     2b
     2c
     3a

EXPLORATION : 7.	Find out what electricity is used for in school. Show your results.

WAYS FORWARD

When the children have completed their survey, they could divide the uses of electricity into categories, eg lighting, heating, power. Each object could then be allocated to its category, and the location noted, to present the findings of the survey as a chart. For example:

Type of use	Objects	Where found
power	computer	classroom
power	television	hall
heating	radiator	staffroom
lighting	fluorescent tubes	classroom

MATERIALS NEEDED AND SAFETY POINTS

- Paper and pens/pencils.
- Clipboard

Safety
- Remind children of the dangers of the mis-use of electricity. They must not touch plug points during their search.

NATIONAL CURRICULUM ASSESSMENT OPPORTUNITIES

Sc 1 / 1a   Sc 4 / 1a
                     3a

MY SCHOOL

EXPLORATION : 8.   Make a collection of as many different kinds of material as you can. Sort out the materials.

WAYS FORWARD

Encourage children to collect as much as possible from around the classroom. If they wish, they could bring additional materials in from home.

Find as many different ways as possible of sorting the items, eg
- made/not made
- liquid/solid
- wood/plastic/metal
- bendy or flexible/rigid or inflexible
- transparent/opaque.

MATERIALS NEEDED AND SAFETY POINTS

- A wide variety of materials from the classroom.

NATIONAL CURRICULUM ASSESSMENT OPPORTUNITIES

Sc 1 / 1a	Sc 3 / 2a
	3a
	3b

GARDENS

- Make a bird table.
- How would you make a butterfly garden?
- Draw an imaginary animal which would be camouflaged in your garden.
- Design and make your own indoor garden.
- Make a winter garden.

FARMING

- Farmers around the world grow different crops and keep different animals. What do they grow and why?

GROW IT OR MAKE IT

PLANTS

- How are all plants the same? How are all plants different?
- Find the best place for a plant to grow.

MATERIALS

- What can we make from various materials?

FUELS

- What can we use as fuels?
- How do we use different fuels?

CROSS CURRICULAR LINKS

Mathematics: Data handling. Sorting plants into groups. Growths of plants over time. Surveys of houseplants/animals in children's homes or classes around the school. Graphing.

History: Has what people eat changed over time? What did Vikings/Romands etc eat? (What did they use for fuel? What did they farm?)
Do your parents eat different foods now than they did 10 years ago?
How has the cooking of foods changed over time?

Geography: What is mined in different parts of Britain/the world? What is farmed in various countries? What firms are there around school? What do they manufacture? Marking main types of farming around Europe/the world on a map.

Technology: Making bird tables/portable greenhouses.
Designing gardens for around the school to make it more attractive. Making artefacts using a variety of materials and looking at the properties of each.

English: **Stories**
Jim and the Beanstalk Raymond Briggs (Puffin)
The Tiny Seed Eric Carle (Knight Books)
Janine and the new baby Iolette Thomas (Andre Deutsch)
You'll soon grow into them, Titch Pat Hutchins (Puffin)

GROW IT OR MAKE IT

| EXPLORATION : 1.   How are all plants the same? How are they different from each other? |

WAYS FORWARD

Give the children as wide a variety of plants as possible, preferably in pots so that roots can be seen. Give them pictures of many other plants. Good plants to include would be cacti, grasses, pine needles, holly, celery, rhododendrons, roses. If the plant produces berries, it would be useful to show these. The plants should include some with narrow, broad and fleshy leaves — also plants with thorns.

Children could compare colour/size/area/shape/width of leaves and also whether any have thorns or stickiness present. The appearance of stems/trunks and roots may also vary. They could extend their studies to shrubs/trees/flowering plants in the school grounds. Classification work could be carried out and results tabulated. Children could also produce keys for friends to identify various plants.

Plants are rooted in one spot and although the colour of chloropyll inside the leaves varies, it generally appears green. Their method of reproduction is usually through seeds/spores (which may be inside a fruit/flower) or by feelers growing from the main plant. Obviously, plants vary according to the conditions they live in — for example, cacti store water and have extensive root systems.

Pupils might investigate how seed dispersal varies throughout the plant world.

MATERIALS NEEDED AND SAFETY POINTS

- A variety of plants and pictures of more unusual / unavailable plants.
- Reference books about processes of plant life, and classification books for trees and flowers (preferably very simple ones).
- Pens, paper, glue for making charts. Drawing paper for drawing plants.
- Magnifying glasses/simple microscopes.
- Peas/bean pods, sycamore seeds, dandelion heads, berries if you wish to discuss seed dispersal.
- Fruits, eg pears, apples, oranges if you wish to look in detail at fruits and their seeds.

Safety
- Children should not put their fingers in or near their mouths when handling leaves/fruits and soil.
- Make sure none of the fruits/berries/ leaves is poisonous, eg rhubarb leaves are poisonous.

NATIONAL CURRRICULUM ASSESSMENT OPPORTUNITIES

Sc 1 / 1a	Sc 1 / 3b	Sc 2 / 1a	Sc 2 / 2c
2a	3c	2a	3a
2b		2b	3c

EXPLORATION : 2.   Find the best places for plants and seeds to grow.

WAYS FORWARD

Children could look inside the school buildings and in the school grounds to see where plants grow, eg on the window sills, window boxes, on walls, in flower beds, between paving stones, etc.

They could plant cress seeds, mustard seeds or mung beans on trays of cotton wool and place them in a variety of positions, eg in a dark cupboard, on a window sill (draughty perhaps), in the middle of the classroom, outside among a flower bed or under a greenhouse, in the shade of a wall, on a pathway/grassy area, between buildings, in a hanging basket (shady or bright and draughty perhaps).

Consider what is needed for plants to grow, ie reasonable temperature (away from draughts), water, light, nutrients.

Children could measure the growth over time, eg length, weight, number of leaves. Try growing bulbs, carrot tops, broad beans, Busy Lizzies or similar. Does the best place to grow vary with the plant chosen?

Children could also make bar charts/data bases to show growth and also where plants are found. Children could also identify some of the parts of plants, eg seed, root, shoot, leaves, flowers.

As an extension, consider whether the appearance of a plant affects where it grows, ie are plants adapted to their environment? For example do plants in shady areas have big leaves, are they shorter, longer, more bushy than those in light areas?

MATERIALS NEEDED AND SAFETY POINTS

- Reference books about care of plants.
- Compost/Soil.
- Seeds and plants, eg cress, mustard, fruit pips, mung or broad beans, carrot/onion/potato tops, Busy Lizzy, geranium.
- Meat trays, margarine containers or similar.
- Cotton wool, tissue paper, magnifying glass, ruler, graph paper.

Safety
- Wash your hands after handling soil.
- Don't eat seeds.

NATIONAL CURRICULUM ASSESSMENT OPPORTUNITIES

Sc 1 / 1a	Sc 1/ 3b	Sc 2 / 1a
2a	3c	1b
2b	3d	2a
2c		2c
3a		2d

GROW IT OR MAKE IT

> ### EXPLORATION : 3. What can you make from these?
>
> ## WAYS FORWARD
>
> Children need a variety of different materials, including those shown on the page.
>
> Looking around the classroom/school they can explore how each material is used, eg:
> Wood — desks/chairs/shelves/cupboards/pencils.
> Wool — jumpers/blankets/felt board.
> Plastic — pipes/chairs/pencil cases/PE hoops/balls.
>
> How has the material been changed from its natural state to make these artefacts? Has it been treated to make it more attractive, eg wood stained or wool dyed?
>
> Discuss with children how different foods change when cooked, eg chocolate, potato, eggs, cheese.
>
> Children can use books and/or interview people to find out how things are manufactured, making charts and databases of all their findings.
>
> As an extension, children could dye wool and other fabrics using natural and manufactured dyes, eg onion skins, beetroot juice, blackcurrant juice, carrots. They could fire clay to make pots/bricks, etc.

MATERIALS NEEDED AND SAFETY POINTS

- A variety of materials such as those shown in the book.
- Reference books about how wood, metals, wool/cotton, etc are processed.
- Large sheets of paper, pens/pencils for making charts.
- A variety of cookery materials and facilities.

NATIONAL CURRICULUM ASSESSMENT OPPORTUNITIES

Sc 1 / 1a	Sc 2 / 1a
2a	2a
2b	2b
2c	3a
3a	3b
3b	
3d	

EXPLORATION : 4.	Why do farmers round the world grow different plants and keep different animals?

WAYS FORWARD

Children will need a variety of reference books to look into what food people eat in different countries, eg hot climates (Africa/India), cold climates (Iceland/Arctic), temperate climates (Europe). Foods which grow best in tropical conditions include tropical fruit, rice, sugar cane, coffee and tea. Wheat, root vegetables, apples, pears, blackcurrants and blackberries all grow well in a temperate climate. In cold climates most of the farming tends to be of animals such as the reindeer and caribou, and fishing.

As a rule, the animals which are farmed tend to be native to the area and adapted to its conditions, eg reindeer in Lapland, camels in Africa.

As part of the children's recording of their information, they could create a display based around a map of the world with pointers from countries attached to children's drawings of animals and plants farmed there.

Children who have relatives in, or have had holidays in, other countries could prove a useful resource.

As an extension, children could make quizzes/games for their friends about farming in other countries. A 20 questions-type game, where they guess the country, could work well.

Pupils could attempt to grow fruit stones normally grown in hot climates, indoors or in a greenhouse, eg peaches, avocados, lime/orange/lemon pips.

MATERIALS NEEDED AND SAFETY POINTS

- A variety of reference books about other countries including hot/cold/temperate climates.
- Paper, pencils, pens, crayons and card.
- Junk for making games.
- A variety of fruits from around the world for children to look at/grow the pips from/decide whereabouts in the world they grow.

Safety
- Do not eat fruit pips.

NATIONAL CURRICULUM ASSESSMENT OPPORTUNITIES

Sc 1 / 1a	Sc 2 / 1b
2b	2a
2c	2b
3a	2c
3c	3a
	3c

GROW IT OR MAKE IT

EXPLORATION : 5.   There are many different fuels. How do we use them? What other fuels can you think of?

WAYS FORWARD

Consider which fuels we use to power objects around the school, eg tape recorder, television, computer, the heating system, the cars in the car park.

Children could also carry out a survey at home of how objects work, eg gas, coal or log fire, electric cooker, oil-fired central heating.

How were coal/gas/oil made? Where do we find them and how are they removed? You could also talk about the conservation of such fuels for future generations.

Ask children to record how frequently each of these fuels is used in school or at home. Where possible, they should look at samples of oil, coal and wood, and see how they burn under controlled conditions — preferably out of doors.

Children could make Venn diagrams showing how household objects are normally powered or create a power scrap book for their house. Both would use childrens' or magazine pictures of appliances.

MATERIALS NEEDED AND SAFETY POINTS

- Reference books about coal, oil, electricity, wood, gas and other fuels, and their formation and processing.
- Graph paper, crayons, pencils.
- Magnifying glasses.
- Samples of coal, oil, wood.

Safety
- Wash your hands after handling the fuels.

NATIONAL CURRICULUM ASSESSMENT OPPORTUNITIES

Sc 1 / 1a	Sc 3 / 1a	Sc 4 / 1a
2b	2b	3a
3d	3b	3b

GROW IT OR MAKE IT

EXPLORATION : 6. Design and make your own indoor garden.

WAYS FORWARD

Children should decide what container they are going to use for their garden, considering, for example, whether it is strong and waterproof. They need to design their garden on paper in pictorial form. Quick-growing plants for such gardens are mustard/cress/mung bean/broad bean.

Children might grow a miniature vegetable garden, or Bonzai garden. Obviously splitting the garden into areas through miniature rockeries or walls would make it look more attractive and segregate the plants. Children might consider plants to add colour and height variation.

Potato, onion and carrot tops could prove useful as cheap plants. (It could be a miniature allotment or spice garden.)

Children could measure the growth of plants and compare them with one another. They could produce charts, bar charts and produce a database comparing plants with one another.

MATERIALS NEEDED AND SAFETY POINTS

- Variety of plastic/pottery/glass containers, eg old plant pots (perhaps decorated), old sinks, bottles.
- Compost, soil, stones, broken pottery — perhaps polystyrene packaging.
- Variety of seeds, plant tops, bulbs, conkers, acorns, fruit pips/stones.
- Magnifying glasses.
- Reference books to find out about seeds to be grown.
- Paper/graph paper.
- Plant labels.

Safety
- Children should be reminded not to eat the seeds.
- It is important to wash hands after handling soil.

NATIONAL CURRICULUM ASSESSMENT OPPORTUNITIES

Sc 1 / 1a	Sc 2 / 1a	Sc 3 / 1a
2a	1b	2a
2b	2a	3a
2c	2b	
3a	2c	
3b	3c	
3c		
3d		

TOPIC: SPACESHIP EARTH

EARTH

•Find out what shape other people think the world is. What are their reasons?

TIME

•Find out how long it takes you to do everyday things, eg dress, tie your shoelace, write your name.
•How long is a second, minute, hour, day, month, year?
•Find out the time using a sundial or a home-made shadow stick.

SPACESHIP EARTH

SUN AND MOON

•How does the Sun change throughout the day? What happens at night?
•What problem would you have planning a trip to the Moon? to the Sun?
•Does the Sun/Moon/length of day change during the year?

WEATHER

•Find out about the changes in the weather over a year.
•Can you keep your own weather chart?
•Does the weather affect your and other animals' behaviour?

CROSS-CURRICULAR LINKS

Geography: Looking at a globe and considering the position of the major continents in relation to one another and the position of Great Britain, what can be seen from space, eg Great Wall of China, Rift Valley (Africa), Grand Canyon?

Technology: Making mobiles and models to show the position of the Earth, Sun and Moon in relation to one another.

Art: Drawing the effects created by light from the Sun on landscape, eg shadows, reflections in lakes.
Watercolour paintings of sunset, showing trees and houses silhouetted against the orange/yellow/red sun.

English: Writing to a pen pal on another planet. Describe a day on Earth. How do you brush your teeth/wash? How do you travel around — bus, car, train, aeroplane? What is a television, stereo music system, cooker? Write a holiday brochure for an alien's holiday to Earth.

Story
A small pinch of weather Joan Aiken (Lutterworth)

EXPLORATION : 1.   Find out the time using a shadow stick you have made.

WAYS FORWARD

It would be useful to bring in a sundial (children would have difficulty making one)The dial should be set in position using a compass.

Children can make a shadow stick or clock by placing a stick into the ground on the playing field or placing a rounders post or some other upright stick on the playground. Such a clock could also be made by the children by glueing or nailing a wooden stick onto a baseboard of some kind. Children could place these near windows around the classroom and note where the shadow falls throughout the day.

They can calibrate their own clocks by noting where the shadow falls with a pencil or chalk at hourly or two-hourly intervals throughout the day. Does the shadow falling on the base vary according to where the shadow clock is placed in the classroom?

Children can compare the divisions and times shown on their clock with that on the sundial. Discussions could result about why the shadow changes throughout the day, ie due to the 'movement' of the Sun.

As an extension children could draw pictures including the Sun and a range of objects such as trees, children and buildings, showing where the shadow of these objects would fall on the ground. Does the length of the shadow change throughout the day? Why?

MATERIALS NEEDED AND SAFETY POINTS

- Pieces of flat wood/corriflute/cardboard for the base.
- Rounders posts or long skittles for the stick.
- Glue, stickytape, nails, hammer, PE hoops, chalk, pencils, watches/clocks.
- Sundial (if possible).

Safety:
- Warn children never to look at the Sun directly.

NATIONAL CURRICULUM ASSESSMENT OPPORTUNITIES

Sc 1 / 1a	Sc 1 / 3b	Sc 4 / 1d
2a	3c	2d
2b	3d	
2c		
3a		

SPACESHIP EARTH

EXPLORATION : 2.	How does the Sun change throughout the day? Find a way to record what you find out.

WAYS FORWARD

Children can chart the passage of the Sun across the sky, either on a window with sticky tape or by noting the shadow cast by a shape on the window on a piece of paper. This should be done at particular times during the day, eg every two hours. The change in position of the Sun across the sky can also be seen by using a tin can and placing light-sensitive (eg photographic) paper on one end and a pin prick in the other (like a pin-hole camera). If this is left where Sun can shine through the hole, a semi-circular trace will be seen due to the movement of the light from the Sun across the paper.

Children can also draw their shadow on their playground by working in pairs. One of them stands in the same spot every 2 hours throughout the day on a sunny day. (The shadow is short at mid-day when the Sun is directly overhead and long in the afternoon.)

Children could discuss why it is dark at night. Can you see the Sun at night — why not? Children could investigate, using books or consulting adults, why it is dark at night. (If the teacher has worked with children on some of the activities at the beginning of this set of explorations, children should understand the reason for 'night' better.)

Children could record their results as pictures, charts or as a 'Sun map' by splitting the window into a grid and marking the position of the Sun on the window as a reference. This could be plotted on a computer screen or read into a tape recorder.

MATERIALS NEEDED AND SAFETY POINTS

- Coloured sticky tape or sticky shapes, white sugar paper, Blu-tack.
- Large cans, sensitive photographic paper, chalk, clocks/watches.

Safety
- Never look directly at the sun. This is particularly relevant in this exploration.

NATIONAL CURRICULUM ASSESSMENT OPPORTUNITIES

Sc 1 / 1a	Sc 4 / 1d
2a	2d
2b	2e
2c	3e (part)
3a	
3b	
3c	
3d	

EXPLORATION : 3.   How does the length of day change through the year? How does the Moon change through the month.

WAYS FORWARD

Recording the Sun/day length

Children could record Sunrise and Sunset every month on the first or last day throughout the year. This information is also available in newspapers throughout the year, in *Whitaker's Almanack* and in some diaries.

This information could be stored in charts, on the computer in database, or on a tape recorder. Children could draw graphs to show Sunrise and Sunset throughout the year.

The highest point of the Sun in the sky is halfway between Sunrise and Sunset.

Alternatively, younger children could monitor whether it is light or dark at particular times during the day on the first or last day of each month, eg at 8.00am and 4.30pm and could then decide whether day length or hours of light varied throughout the year.

Recording the change in position of the Sun over the year, could consist of marking the position of the Sun on a large window, or the shadow of a shape on the window, at the same time, — eg midday on the first or last day of each month over a year. This could be stored as a grid reference on a computer if the window were split into a simple grid.

Recording the Moon

The appearance of the Moon changes at different times during each month, but not over a year. Children could start their observations at either the new Moon or the beginning of a month. They could prepare a chart to fill in each evening at the same time. The chart could show the shape of the Moon and the position in which it can be seen on the window each evening. The chart could be in picture form, ie picking out the major features seen from the window and drawing them in a silhouette, then marking the position and shape of the Moon relative to them.

Children could also chart the Moon at a set time during the day, when possible, to see whether the shape and/or position varies at that time over the month/year, and whether it differs from their evening observations. Younger children might take an observation only twice weekly.

MATERIALS NEEDED AND SAFETY POINTS

- Paper, pencil, crayons, diary, daily newspapers, coloured sticky labels, sugar paper (preferably white), *Whitakers Almanack*, graph paper, clock/watch.

NATIONAL CURRICULUM ASSESSMENT OPPORTUNITIES

Sc 1 / 1a	Sc 1 / 3b	Sc 4 / 1d
2a	3c	2e
2b	3d	3e
2c		
3a		

SPACESHIP EARTH

EXPLORATION : 4.   How does the weather change through the year?

WAYS FORWARD

Obviously, if children take note of the weather every day over a school year, the data collected would be difficult to handle. Making a record on one day each week is easier. The children should be encouraged to use weather symbols, researched from newspapers, television or reference books. They could use these symbols as a basis for creating their own. Magnetic or felt board charts could be used with paper clips or sandpaper backs respectively, on the symbols.

Perhaps children could show the weather each month on such a board before transferring it to the year's chart. Databases could also be created on the computer, especially ones which could graph or chart the results. Children could make rain gauges to record the rainfall or snowfall on the day to be measured, or anemometers. The cloud cover could also be noted by calculating the proportion of a window which has clouds in it (a large window works best).

At the end of each season and/or at the end of the year, children can draw bar charts to show the frequency of each type of weather.

Class discussion about how the type of weather affects people's lives could be an extension activity. Children might produce Spring/Summer/Autumn/Winter charts showing the most frequent types of weather and clothing worn in each season. Does weather affect the type of activities/sports people do throughout the year? Does it affect the food we eat?

Children could record the sounds of weather such as rain, hail and thunder and reproduce the sounds on musical instruments.

MATERIALS NEEDED AND SAFETY POINTS

- Large sheet of paper/card.
- Fabric, card, beads, glue, gummed paper, scraps of coloured paper, felt and crayons/felt tips to make the weather symbols.
- Sticky or double-sided tape to stick on symbols.
- Rulers.

NATIONAL CURRICULUM ASSESSMENT OPPORTUNITIES

Sc 1 / 1a
        2a
        2b
        2c
        3a
        3b
        3c
        3d

EXPLORATION : 5.   Find out what shape people think our planet Earth is. What are their reasons for thinking this?

WAYS FORWARD

Children could use videos, books, newspapers, television and other people (including relatives) to investigate what shape people think the world is.

The result might be a folder of evidence. This could be newspaper articles, photographs, drawings, pictures, writing and tapes/transcripts of interviews. The children could split into groups, each producing a presentation to perform to other groups, to justify their conclusions as to the Earth's shape.

Reasons why people believe the Earth is round might include:
1) If one travels in the same direction around the Earth, one eventually returns to where one started.
2) The shadow of the Earth cast on the Moon is round. (The phases of the Moon are due to the fact that the shadow of the Earth on the Moon changes over a month.)
3) Photographs of Earth from space show it to be a sphere.
4) Astronauts returning from space have reported that they saw a sphere rotating in space.

MATERIALS NEEDED AND SAFETY POINTS

- Reference books/charts/posters on astronomy, containing diagrams and photographs of the Solar system.
- Old newspaper articles about journeys into space and photographs produced.
- Videos, TV programmes about astronomy.
- Children's story books about space travel.

NATIONAL CURRICULUM ASSESSMENT OPPORTUNITIES

Sc 1 / 1a	Sc 4 / 1d
2a	2e
2b	
3d	

SPACESHIP EARTH

EXPLORATION : 6.   Show somebody else why it gets dark at night.

WAYS FORWARD

Children should have an awareness of how the planets are arranged around the Sun and that the Earth spins on its axis. Carrying out the following activity will help the children.

Shine a torch on a globe. Spin it and talk about how we get night and day as the earth spins - the sun stays still and at night Britain is pointing away from the Sun and therefore is dark.

As an extension, try this, using an electric lamp to represent the Sun and a globe to represent the Earth. Move the globe around the lamp so that it orbits the lamp in the same way that the Earth orbits the Sun. Observe closely how the lamp shines on the globe when it is in different positions during its orbit. This should help children begin to understand the concept of the seasons.

The children could write a story about the time when no night came — perhaps the Earth stopped spinning (the axis needed oiling!!) or an alien/giant from space stopped it! Or alternatively the Sun was switched off for a reason or refused to shine?

MATERIALS NEEDED AND SAFETY POINTS

- Globes, torches, standard lamp, variety of sizes of balls.
- Old coathangers for mobiles, variety of colours of card (perhaps cut in a variety of circular sizes).
- Long sports tape measure.
- Paper, pencils, tape recorders.

NATIONAL CURRICULUM ASSESSMENT OPPORTUNITIES

Sc 1 / 1a	Sc 4 / 1d
2a	2e
2b	3e
2c	
3a	
3b	
3d	

EXPLORATION : 7.   Plan a trip to the Moon. What problems might there be? Plan a trip to the Sun. What problems might there be?

WAYS FORWARD

A chart of the Solar system would be useful. Children will have to consider the distance to each of these places - they are a long way away and up in space, so a rocket with a large quantity of fuel would be needed. The Moon is nearer than the Sun, so less fuel would be required for that trip.

Children need to consider the environments they are likely to find on each, and how different they would be from Earth and from one another. (How different they are from one another needs to be reiterated.) Splitting the class into groups — one visiting the Sun and one the Moon — may be appropriate.

What extra equipment would be required given the conditions? — eg on the Moon there is little oxygen, less gravity, no water and therefore no food, and it is very rocky. Children could make charts to show comparisons between the Sun and the Moon. They will need to consider things they would have to take which are necessary for life, and give reasons for each (See also Exploration 4 in Journey into Space *Exploring Science Book 1*). They should consider what is necessary to keep healthy, eg exercise, medicines.

Children could produce a Sun Exploration Kit and a Moon Exploration Kit, containing models of what they would need to take and of their Space vehicle. They could rate the contents in order of importance.

The time element in getting to each should be considered - it is more than a day trip!

As an extension, children could write the story of their trips to the Sun or the Moon and possible adventures they might have. Wherever possible, this should be based on facts learnt from research. Look also into myths and legends, eg Icarus, who flew too close to the Sun and melted his wings.

MATERIALS NEEDED AND SAFETY POINTS

- Reference books/newspapers, posters, videos, films on the Sun, Moon and space travel.
- Old boxes, cardboard rolls, yoghurt pots etc for modelling.
- Glue, sticky tape, sugar paper, writing and drawing paper.

NATIONAL CURRICULUM ASSESSMENT OPPORTUNITIES

Sc 1 / 2a	Sc 2 / 2a	Sc 4 / 1d
2b	3a	2e
		3e

TOPIC: PARTY TIME

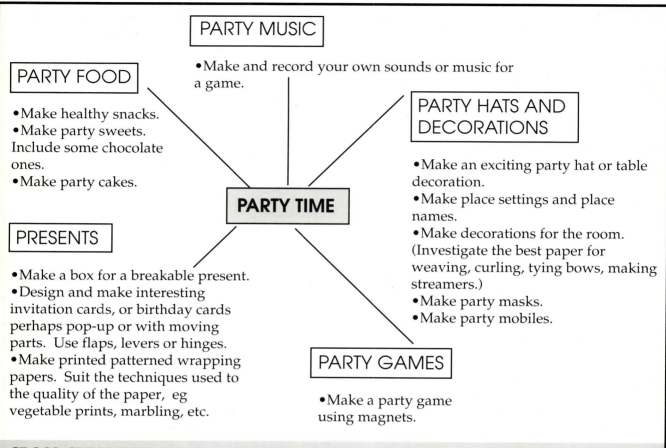

PARTY MUSIC
- Make and record your own sounds or music for a game.

PARTY FOOD
- Make healthy snacks.
- Make party sweets. Include some chocolate ones.
- Make party cakes.

PARTY HATS AND DECORATIONS
- Make an exciting party hat or table decoration.
- Make place settings and place names.
- Make decorations for the room. (Investigate the best paper for weaving, curling, tying bows, making streamers.)
- Make party masks.
- Make party mobiles.

PARTY TIME

PRESENTS
- Make a box for a breakable present.
- Design and make interesting invitation cards, or birthday cards perhaps pop-up or with moving parts. Use flaps, levers or hinges.
- Make printed patterned wrapping papers. Suit the techniques used to the quality of the paper, eg vegetable prints, marbling, etc.

PARTY GAMES
- Make a party game using magnets.

CROSS-CURRICULAR LINKS

Mathematics: Data handling — graphing of favourite party foods or   favourite party game.

Technology: Design and make cards, hats, presents, menus for the party.

English: **Stories:**
Mrs Wobble, the waitress , Allan Ahlberg (Puffin)
Charlie and the chocolate factory, Roald Dahl (Puffin)
The trouble with Jack, Shirley Hughes (Picture Lion)
The pudding like a night on the sea from *The Julian Stories*, Ann Cameron (Fontana Young Lions)
Poems:
Sweet Song/Party piece/If your roly poly jelly/Happy birthday card from *A Very First Poetry Book* compiled by John Foster (OUP)

EXPLORATION : 1.   Make some healthy snacks. Think of some good names for them.

WAYS FORWARD

Discuss with children which foods they consider healthy — and introduce children to foods they may not be familiar with. Visit a supermarket for ideas.

Vegetable snacks:
Tomato, cucumber, lettuce, watercress. carrots, celery, radish, cauliflower — serve alone or with peanut butter or cottage cheese.
Try making guacamole (puree tomato, avocado; add grated onion with lemon juice, plus chilli powder, salt and black pepper to taste).

Dried fruit snacks and grains:
Raisins, apricots, dates, dried apples or pears.
Different nuts and seeds.
Unsweetened coconut.
Wholegrain bread and crackers (not caramel coloured).
Try baking bread, using flours from whole grains.
Dry cereals — choose unsweetened varieties like shredded wheat, 100% Bran. Try adding natural yoghurt to fruit and cereals.

Fresh fruit snacks:
Apples, bananas, berries, cherries, grapes, melons, oranges, peaches, plums, pears, etc. Make a fruit salad using these.
For the syrup, dissolve castor sugar in hot water, add lemon juice or orange juice to taste.
Alternatively, try a fizzy fruit punch — mixing fruit with unsweetened fresh orange juice and lemonade, and adding ice cubes and sprigs of mint.

Drinks:
Use fruit juices and tomato juice instead of fruit drinks. Serve milk plain or blended with banana or other fruit, orange juice and ice for a healthy milkshake.
Fruity milk shake: for 8 guests you will need 2 litres (3 pints) milk, 500g (1lb) soft fruit (eg bananas, strawberries) 3 tablespoons sugar. Prepare the fruit — peel and take out any stones. Mash the fruit with a fork, then whisk it into the milk with the sugar.

As an extension children could design their own party menu.

MATERIALS NEEDED AND SAFETY POINTS

• Food ingredients as above.

Safety
• Take care with nuts and seeds — children can choke on them.

NATIONAL CURRICULUM ASSESSMENT OPPORTUNITIES

Sc 1 / 1a   Sc 2 / 2a (food)   Sc 3 / 1a
      2a   2b
      2b

PARTY TIME

> ### EXPLORATION : 2.   Make some party sweets. Include some chocolate ones.

WAYS FORWARD

Allow children to experiment with the ingredients so that they understand why quantities are specified. For example, give them the ingredients of coconut ice and ask them to work out the right quantities by actually mixing them together.

Recipe: uncooked sweets
Coconut ice
Ingredients: 250g desiccated coconut
                    250g icing sugar
                    Small tin condensed milk
                    Food colouring
1. Sieve the icing sugar into a bowl and mix it thoroughly with the coconut.
2. Little by little, add the condensed milk and mix it well with a wooden spoon. Add food colouring.
3. Put the mixture, which should be very stiff, onto a lightly oiled board and roll it out until it is about 2.5 cm thick.
4. Leave it overnight to harden and then cut it into cubes.

Recipe: cooked sweets
Butterscotch
Ingredients: 1/4 pt water
                    450g demerara sugar
                    50g butter
1. Pour water into pan and bring to boil.
2. Add sugar and butter, heat slowly, stirring until sugar dissolves and butter melts.
3. Bring to the boil. Cover pan. Boil gently for 2 mins.
4. Uncover. Continue to boil without stirring for about 12 minutes (or until a little piece of the mixture, dropped into a cup of cold water, separates into hard, brittle threads).
5. Pour into buttered 15cm square tin.
6. Mark into squares or bars when almost set, with a buttered knife. Break up when hard, and wrap in waxed paper.

Other suggestions: Chocolate rice krispies, jellies, chocolate cakes, peppermint creams, ice cream sundaes with ice cream, fresh fruit and chocolate sauce made with melted plain chocolate. (Break 125g of plain chocolate into a bowl with 3 tablespoons of water, stand it over a pan of simmering water until it melts.)

MATERIALS NEEDED AND SAFETY POINTS

- Food ingredients as above.

Safety
- Careful supervision is necessary when children are involved in heating and cooking substances.

NATIONAL CURRICULUM ASSESSMENT OPPORTUNITIES

Sc 1 / 1a	Sc 3 / 1a	Sc 3 / 3a
2a	2a	
2b	2b	

EXPLORATION: 3.   Make bread

WAYS FORWARD

Here is a basic recipe for white bread.

Ingredients:
15floz (425ml) hot water
1 tsp white sugar
2 level tsp dried yeast
$1^1/_2$ lb (700g) string white flour
1 level tbs salt
$^1/_2$ oz (10g) butter

1. Butter the insides of two 1lb(450g) loaf tins.
2. Pour the 150ml water into a bowl, whisk in the sugar then the yeast. Put to one side.
3. Sift the flour and salt into a bowl and rub in the butter.
4. Make a well in the centre and pour in the frothy yeast mixture and the rest of the water.
5. Mix with a wooden spoon until the mixture starts to bind together, then use hands to make it into a dough.
6. Knead the dough on a flat surface for about 10 minutes or until it is blistering under the surface.
7. Cover the dough and leave to rise until it is about twice the size (about 1-2 hours at room temperature).
8. Knead the dough again for 5 minutes, then divide in half making each half an oblong shape.
9. Fold the two ends into the centre, one on top of the other.
10. Put each one into a tin, dust with flour and put them into an oiled polythene bag until the dough comes above the top of the tins (about an hour at room temperature).
11. Bake for about 35-40 minutes in the oven, gas mark 8, 230° C.
12. Turn out and leave to cool on a wire rack.

Please note that the recipe shown in the children's book should read $1^1/_2$lb strong white flour.

MATERIALS NEEDED AND SAFETY POINTS

• Ingredients as above.

Safety
• Take care near cookers and electricity.

NATIONAL CURRICULUM ASSESSMENT OPPORTUNITIES

Sc 1 / 1a	Sc 3 / 1a
2a	2b
2b	
2c	
3a	
3b	
3d	

PARTY TIME

EXPLORATION : 4.   Make an exciting party hat or table decoration.

WAYS FORWARD

Make available a wide range of materials.

Some suggestions for things to make:

Hats:
Apart from the usual paper and card hats, children can make hats with moving parts — eg by pulling a string or elastic thread a false hand waves!

Children can use simple circuits for a hat which lights up or one with a motorised spinner — securely fixed, of course.

Coloured acetates can be used so that the hat appears different from each direction.

Table Decorations:
Mini lanterns using simple electric circuits.
Clay decorations/candle holders.
Candles fixed in empty bottles with a 'dripped wax' effect down the sides.

MATERIALS NEEDED AND SAFETY POINTS

• As wide a range of materials as possible. Include wax candles and clay and electric circuits.

Safety
• Take care with the use of lit candles and electricity — definitely no mains electricity!

NATIONAL CURRICULUM ASSESSMENT OPPORTUNITIES

Sc 1 / 1a	Sc 3 / 1a	Sc 4 / 1a
2a	2a	3a
2b	3a	
2c		
3d		

EXPLORATION : 5.   Make a party game which uses magnets.

WAYS FORWARD

Give children a variety of magnets and ask them to find out what the magnets can pick up, or which objects the magnets can attract or repel.

Game suggestions:

- The strongest magnet!
  From a selection of magnets, can children predict which magnet could pick up the most paper clips?

- Catch the biggest fish!
  Make a simple fishing rod with magnets attached to the lines and use these to pick up 'fish' peppered with paper clips. Who can catch the biggest fish/most fish within a time limit?

- World's most difficult maze!
  Map out an interesting maze. Can children trace a metal object through the winding routes of the maze, using a magnet under the board?

MATERIALS NEEDED AND SAFETY POINTS

- A variety of magnets.
- Materials for making games, eg card, paper, sticky tape.
- A variety of magnetic and non-magnetic objects

NATIONAL CURRICULUM ASSESSMENT OPPORTUNITIES

Sc 1 / 1a	Sc 2 / 2a	Sc 4 / 2a
	2b	
	3a	
	3d	

PARTY TIME

> ## EXPLORATION : 6.   Make and test a box for a breakable present. Make it look good.
>
> ### WAYS FORWARD
>
> Discuss with the children what the breakable present might be. They could choose their own — but remind them that the size of the box must be appropriate to the size/shape of the present!
>
> Make available a wide variety of materials — tissue, crepe paper, card of various thicknesses, polythene, fabric, corriflute, polystyrene.
>
> Allow the children to search the classroom for boxes and to undo a box to see how it folds together. Make available a variety of fixing agents, eg sticky tape, glue.   The box must not collapse!
>
> Devise a strength test, eg dropping a weight on the box, or dropping the box from a certain height.
>
> Encourage children to think about padding the box to prevent the present from moving around.
>
> As an extension, the children could wrap the box, making the wrapping as attractive as they can.

MATERIALS NEEDED AND SAFETY POINTS

- Materials as above.
- Objects to represent breakable presents.

NATIONAL CURRICULUM ASSESSMENT OPPORTUNITIES

Sc 1 / 1a	Sc 3 / 1a
2a	2a
2b	3a
2c	
3a	
3b	
3c	
3d	

EXPLORATION : 7.   Make and record your own music for Pass the Parcel.

WAYS FORWARD

Encourage children to combine using manufactured musical instruments — recorder, xylophone, tambourine, triangles, etc — with home-made ones, eg milk bottles, tin can drums, yoghurt pot shakers, elastic band guitars !

Children could also sing and add mixed snippets of their favourite records and tapes — depending on the availability of more than one tape recorder.

MATERIALS NEEDED AND SAFETY POINTS

- Tape recorder, with microphone if available, and tapes.
- Yoghurt pots, beans, lentils.
- Tin cans.
- Polythene.
- Milk bottles.
- Elastic bands, pieces of wood.
- Sticky tape.

NATIONAL CURRICULUM ASSESSMENT OPPORTUNITIES

Sc 1 / 1a	Sc 3 / 1a	Sc 4 / 1c (part)
2a	2a	3d (part)
2b	3a	
2c		
3a		
3d		

TOPIC: LIGHT FANTASTIC

LIGHT AND COLOUR

•How many different colours can you make? (Think of using dyes, paints, crayons, spinning colours, coloured lights.
•Make a light that changes colour (use of coloured acetate or cellophane).

LIGHT SOURCES

•Light up a dark room in as many different ways as you can.
•Electric light — make a model that uses light bulbs.

COLOUR IN THE ENVIRONMENT

•Sort things into colour groups.

LIGHT FANTASTIC

LIGHT AND SHADOW

•Make a shadow story.
•Make a 'Sun picture' using photographic paper.
Place object on photographic paper and leave for about a day. Remove object and place paper in diluted fixer for 1 minute to preserve image. (An excellent reference is *Ilford Classroom Photography* from Ilford UK Sales, 14-22 Tottenham Street, London, WIP 0AH.)

LIGHT AND MIRRORS

•Make and change pictures using mirrors.

CROSS-CURRICULAR LINKS

Mathematics and IT:	Collating information for database, eg *Our facts* database (BBC computer) for eye colour.
Mathematics:	Investigations with mirrors — shape and symmetry.
Religious Education:	Significance and symbolism of light in RE, eg: Christianity — Creation (Genesis), Christ the Light of the World (St John 1), Birth of Christ following the star, Paschal Candle, Christingle, Noah and the Rainbow; Judaism — Hanukkah; Hinduism — Diwali. Biblical stories/History: Story of Joseph, Jesus curing the blind man, Helen Keller, Samuel Morse.
English:	**Stories** *The bad babies' book of colours* Tony Bradman (Arrow Books) *Annette/Another, another, another and more/Make a bigger puddle/Make a smaller worm*, from *A mirror book* Marion Walter (Andre Deutsch) *Patrick*, Quentin Blake (Picture Puffin) *The mixed-up chameleon* Eric Carle (Picture Puffin) *But where is the green parrot?* Thomas and Wanda Zacharias (Piper Books) *Hugo and the man who stole colours*, Tony Ross (Macmillan)

LIGHT FANTASTIC

EXPLORATION : 1.   Sort things into colours.   How can colours help?

WAYS FORWARD

This activity is specifically designed to encourage children to be aware of the range of colours that exist, both in the natural environment and the manufactured environment.

Encourage children to:
1 make colour collections both from objects within the classroom and from outside, eg shells, stones, grasses, leaves.
2 photograph different coloured plants and to sort photographs. What colours are the most common?
3 make surveys, eg of colours of cars passing the school or of colours of local road signs/symbols.

Encourage the use of block graphs to record results, or a database such as *Our facts* used with a BBC microcomputer.

As an extension, after sorting colours and with the aid of reference books/materials, help children to understand the use of colour in the environment, eg our use of red as a warning colour (from road signs to traffic lights), camouflaged animals such as the green caterpillar which hides from predators, or those camouflaged such as the leopard so that its 'kill' finds it hard to see it, or animals that use their bright colouring to suggest that they are poisonous or to frighten off predators (the 'eyes' of the hawk-eyed moth's wings). A useful reference is Althea's Nature Series — *Animal camouflage* (Dinosaur Publications Ltd).

Flowers also use bright colours to attract pollinating insects such as bees, which go to the flowers to collect nectar and at the same time, by brushing against pollen, transfer it from one flower to another, enabling pollination to take place. Pollination means the transfer of pollen from the stamens of one flower to the stigma, usually of another of the same kind.

MATERIALS NEEDED AND SAFETY POINTS

• A wide variety of coloured objects / materials, and books on camouflage.

Safety:
• Emphasise the need for care outdoors, particularly road safety.

NATIONAL CURRICULUM ASSESSMENT OPPORTUNITIES

Sc 1 / 1a   Sc 2 / 2b   Sc 3 / 1a
         2b

LIGHT FANTASTIC

EXPLORATION : 2.   Act out a shadow story.

WAYS FORWARD

Encourage children to think of and try different ways in which they can make shadows — outside on a sunny day, inside using a white board/screen and the overhead projector, or a torch.

Encourage them to draw round each other's silhouettes and to draw objects and their shadows.

Make moving shadow shapes using hands and objects. Make up a story from the moving shadows.

MATERIALS NEEDED AND SAFETY POINTS

- White board/wall or screen.
- Overhead projector.
- Paper, pens, pencils for drawing.

Safety
- Do not look up at the Sun or into the light of the overhead projector.

NATIONAL CURRICULUM ASSESSMENT OPPORTUNITIES

Sc 1 / 1a   Sc 4 / 1c (part)
    2a   2d (part)
    2b
    3a
    3d

EXPLORATION : 3.   Make a model that uses lights.

WAYS FORWARD

Give children activities so that they become competent at making simple circuits — using insulated wire, bulbs in or out of bulb holders, and batteries. Encourage them both to think of their own experiences and to search in magazines for things that use lights — from lighthouses, dolls' houses, car headlights, traffic and street lights, to bow ties that light up and model monsters with electric eyes!

Make a model:
If there is access to a control box which may be attached to a computer (such as Barnet Control IC, or Lego control box) children could attach their model to this and write simple programmes for operating their model.

MATERIALS NEEDED AND SAFETY POINTS

- Bulbs, bulb holders, wire strippers, batteries, insulated wire, control box if available.
- Junk or re-usable materials sorted out into separate containers, eg container for lolly sticks, one for materials suitable for wheels, etc.
- Glue/sticky tape. Blu-tack is useful for keeping wires attached to batteries.

Safety
- Remind children on no account to place wires into electricity sockets. They should only use batteries or the control box.

NATIONAL CURRICULUM ASSESSMENT OPPORTUNITIES

Sc 1 / 1a	Sc 3 / 1a	Sc 4 / 1c (part)
2a		3a
2b		
3a		
3d		

LIGHT FANTASTIC

EXPLORATION : 4.   Make a picture using mirrors.

WAYS FORWARD

Encourage children to draw pictures and change them by placing a mirror across them and moving the mirror, eg:
- Make a worm longer or shorter.
- Make a river longer or shorter.
- Complete half-done faces or objects.

Place two mirrors together at an angle of about 60°. Make a pattern on a circle of paper. Move this circle of paper beneath the two mirrors, round and round — and watch the change of image.

Make a simple kaleidoscope:
Tape three small mirrors together to resemble a triangular prism.
Place tracing paper (translucent paper) at one end and attach.
Drop beads or small sequins down and attach clear cellophane or cling film to the other end.
Look down and turn your home-made kaleidoscope.

As an extension, make a collection of objects other than mirrors that give a reflection, eg spoons, shiny dark plastic, etc.

Try using mirrors to change the direction of light, eg shine a torchlight on a mirror or mirrors. (This is best done in a dark room.)

MATERIALS NEEDED AND SAFETY POINTS

- Paper, felts and other drawing instruments.
- Beads, sequins, tracing paper, clear cellophane.
- Mirrors.
- Simple slits in small blocks of wood make good mirror stands.

Safety
- Use plastic rather than glass mirrors.
- Wrap masking tape round any sharp edges.

NATIONAL CURRICULUM ASSESSMENT OPPORTUNITIES

Sc 1 / 1a	Sc 4 / 1c (part)
2a	3d (part)
2b	
2c	
3a	
3d	

EXPLORATION : 5.   How many different colours can you make?

WAYS FORWARD

Encourage children to think of all the different media that can be used for colour mixing — from paints, crayons, felts, pencils, to food dyes. Think of how many shades of one colour can be made. Home-made dyes can be made out of food substances — try using turmeric, coffee, tea, blackberries, boiled red cabbage leaves or onion skins. Fold and dip strong kitchen paper or paper towels into dyes, then unfold and observe the results. Dylon cold water dyes can also be used.

Mix coloured lights using different coloured acetate sheets (acetate sheets tend to work better than cellophane). Tape sheets over torches and experiment!

Separate out colours (chromatography) by blobbing colours on blotting paper or coffee filter paper and adding water drops to the colours.

Spin multi-coloured circles and observe the results. Colours will merge to a whitish shade. Attaching coloured discs to a motor makes spinning easy.

NOTE:
Primary colours of paint are red, yellow, blue
Red + yellow = orange
Yellow + blue = green
Red + blue = purple

Red + yellow + blue = brown
Primary colours of light are red, green, blue
Green + blue = cyan blue (greeny blue light)
Blue + red = magenta
Green + red = yellow
Green + red + blue = white

MATERIALS NEEDED AND SAFETY POINTS

- Paints, crayons and dyes as above — as many different colouring tools as possible.
- Variety of papers for colour mixing.
- Circuits for spinning coloured discs — small motors with push-fit pulley attachments, insulated wire, batteries.

NATIONAL CURRICULUM ASSESSMENT OPPORTUNITIES

Sc 1 / 1a	Sc 3 / 1a	Sc 4 / 1a
2a	3b	3a
2b		
2c		
3a		
3d		

LIGHT FANTASTIC

EXPLORATION : 6.   Light up a dark room in as many different ways as you can.

WAYS FORWARD

If possible, black out a room or use the darkest room or stock cupboard.

Encourage children to think of the range of options from daylight (Sun) to electric light to candle light, to combinations of these, including mirrors to reflect available light.

Encourage the making of comparisons, eg Which candle was best?

MATERIALS NEEDED AND SAFETY POINTS

- Matches, variety of candles - all shapes and sizes.
- Circuits and bulbs.
- Curtains or cloth to black out an area or room.

Safety
- Great care is needed with candle flames.
- Discuss the safe use of electricity.

NATIONAL CURRICULUM ASSESSMENT OPPORTUNITIES

Sc 1 / 1a	Sc 4 / 1a
2a	1c (part)
2b	3a
2c	3d (part)
3a	
3d	

SCIENCE THEMES

EARTH, ATMOSPHERE AND SPACE

INTRODUCING THE RESOURCE

THEME BOOK	**What can you do?**
HOW TO USE	Anytime, anywhere. To be read alone or as a shared experience with an adult and/or with friends.

ACTIVITIES AND TEACHER'S BACKGROUND INFORMATION

ACTIVITIES IN THE BOOK

• Discuss the weather conditions portrayed.

• Watch out for the deliberate mistakes! Discuss why they are wrong.

• Rain. Misty windows and condensation.

• Sun. Shadows and rainbows.

• Wind.

• Mist.

• Thunder and lightning.

• Snow and ice.

• Draw weather pictures for yesterday, today and tomorrow.

BACKGROUND INFORMATION

The deliberate mistakes shown in the book are:
Cover: Roses and butterfly in Winter.
Page 1: Petals in Winter.
Page 2: Penguin on beach.
Page 3: Chair leg missing.
Page 4: Snowman in Summer.
Page 5: Boy has two shadows.

EXTENSION ACTIVITIES

• Talk about seasonal weather. What are the seasons? When are they? How many months in a season?

• Talk about sports and games played in different seasons. Where and when would you ski/fly a kite/sunbathe? Would you use a hose?

• Discuss today's weather and the clothing you are wearing. Is it suitable for another time of the year? What functions does our clothing perform?

• When is your shadow longest/shortest? Why? When is it not there? Why? Can you reflect light? How?

• Make your own weather symbols.

• What happens to rain/ice/snow kept indoors? Where does the water evaporate to?

• Talk about what you do in storms, on hot days, etc.

• Adults, too, are affected by the weather — it can affect their jobs — talk about sailors and fishermen.

• Wrapping up (insulating) snow and ice prolongs their form. Water evaporates.

EARTH, ATMOSPHERE AND SPACE

Page 6:   Sheep in boots.
Page 7:   Sunbather in Autumn.
Page 8/9:   Apples on horse chestnut; wind direction.
Page 10:   Cactus.
Page 11:   Lock on wrong side of gate.
Page 12:   Skier on roof.
Page 13:   Teapot spout upside down.
Page 14:   Car through upstairs window.
Page 15:   Upside-down house number, and at the back of the house (two on this page; none on page 16).

MATERIALS NEEDED AND SAFETY POINTS

- Pictures/clothes/photographs of clothing.
- Artifacts for use in a variety of weather conditions.

Safety
- Never look directly at the Sun.

NATIONAL CURRICULUM ASSESSMENT OPPORTUNITIES

Sc 1 / 1a	Sc 2 / 2a	Sc 3 / 2b	Sc 4 / 1d
2a	2c		2b
2b			2d
3a			3d

CROSS-CURRICULAR AND EVERYDAY LINKS

English: Poems, rhymes, stories about the weather/involving weather, eg *The Snowman*, Raymond Briggs.
               Tongue-twisters.

Geography: Weather in different places.

Mathematics: Keep a diary/chart/block graph about the weather.

Art and craft: Use a variety of equipment to make weather pictures. Make a seasonal collage. Look at pictures: what could you do in the places shown in different weather?

Music: Make music about a variety of weather. What sounds would you hear on a rainy day/windy day, etc? Would the Sun have a sound?

History: What did your mother/father do on a rainy day when they were young?

Technology: IT for recording information. Devise a wind gauge. Make something to move in the wind. Blow water up a slope.

EARTH, ATMOSPHERE AND SPACE

INTRODUCING THE RESOURCE

THEME BOOK	**The filthy dirty book**
HOW TO USE	Anytime, anywhere.

ACTIVITIES AND TEACHER'S BACKGROUND INFORMATION

ACTIVITIES IN THE BOOK

- Observation and discussion about the pictures in the book. What types of litter are there? Where does litter come from? Where does litter collect? Why?

- What is pollution? Can you always see pollution?

- Look around your school or your street. Is there any rubbish?

- Ways of improving our environment.

- Talk about recycling. What does it mean?

EXTENSION ACTIVITIES

- Make a litter collection. Sort it out. What was found? How did the litter get there? Why?

- What are the effects of pollution in water/on the ground/in the air?

- Is litter collected in the classroom different from that in the playground? How? Why?

- How can we stop poisoning our environment? Can **you** make a difference?

- Keep a diary of litter decay.

BACKGROUND INFORMATION

- Litter collects because people drop it or dump it, and because plants, etc decay.

- Litter collects because the wind blows it into corners/against barriers — natural or made.

- Litter pollutes rivers, rock pools, ponds, etc, causing obstructions as well as poisoning the environment.

- Animals can be caught and cut by tins and glass.

- Some litter does not decay as quickly as other litter, and some not at all.

EARTH, ATMOSPHERE AND SPACE

MATERIALS NEEDED AND SAFETY POINTS

• A carrier bag, preferably paper, for litter collection.

Safety
• Gloves should be worn when handling litter.
• Do not collect glass.
• Wash hands after making the collection.

NATIONAL CURRICULUM ASSESSMENT OPPORTUNITIES

Sc 1 / 2a   Sc 2 / 2d
    2b   3b
    3d

CROSS-CURRICULAR AND EVERYDAY LINKS

English: Talking and listening, which could be used as a basis for imaginative writing/ poems/recording personal observations.

Geography: Making maps to show where litter collects.

History: Litter past and present. How do we know about past litter?

Mathematics: Sorting and setting.
Block charts.
Prediction of place/mass.
Time : Via a diary and making a bio-degradable area.

Craft: A litter collage.

Technology: Can you design a litter picker?

Art: Designing posters to encourage others to clean up litter.

EARTH, ATMOSPHERE AND SPACE

INTRODUCING THE RESOURCE

THEME BOOK	**Life is a cycle**
HOW TO USE	Anytime, anywhere. Particularly appropriate as part of a seasons topic.

ACTIVITIES AND TEACHER'S BACKGROUND INFORMATION

ACTIVITIES IN THE BOOK

- Discuss the seasons of the year through looking at the pictures. How do you know it is Winter/Spring/Summer/Autumn?

- Daytime and night. "Long" and "short" days.

- Storing food for use during the Winter.

- Wood as a fuel for cooking and keeping warm.

- Hibernation.

- Nuts and seeds.

- Sowing, growing and harvesting.

- Why are the birds hungry?

- Life goes round and round. How do you know this from looking at the pictures?

- Look for natural/made things in the book.

EXTENSION ACTIVITIES

- Make a collection of natural objects to show the current season. Talk about day/night length throughout the year.

- Design a feeder for birds.

- Grow bulbs/plants from seeds. Name the main parts. What is necessary to sustain life, grow and reproduce plants?

- Look for plant growth or signs of animals around the school.

- What can be made from wool? Gather some if possible and consider what can be done with it.

- Investigate similarities and differences between living things.

BACKGROUND INFORMATION

- Some birds stay in the British Isles all year, others migrate to warmer climates.
- If the weather stays cold enough, squirrels will hibernate.

EARTH, ATMOSPHERE AND SPACE

NATIONAL CURRICULUM ASSESSMENT OPPORTUNITIES

Sc 1 / 1a	Sc 2 / 1b	Sc 4 / 1d
2a	2a	2b
2b	2b	3e
2c	2c	
3a	3a	
3b	3b	
3c	3c	
3d		

CROSS-CURRICULAR AND EVERYDAY LINKS

English: Talking, listening, rhymes, stories. Recording observations.

Mathematics: Sorting, setting, recording findings via bar charts, etc.

History: Weather from times past, using old newspapers, pictures and older people's spoken (and recorded) recollections.

Art and Craft: Making artefacts from a wide variety of media.

Technology: Using IT to collect information.

Music and Movement: Make a song for a season.
Move like autumn leaves, a snowman, an animal.

EARTH, ATMOSPHERE AND SPACE

INTRODUCING THE RESOURCE

THEME BOOK

HOW TO USE

Passing time

Conceptually a high level book. Probably best used in small doses.

ACTIVITIES AND TEACHER'S BACKGROUND INFORMATION

ACTIVITIES IN THE BOOK

- Food is a source of energy, ie a fuel. It helps keep us warm.
- Thick clothes help keep the warmth in but they do not give us energy.
- The Sun is a source of energy. It also helps keep us warm.
- All animal and plant life needs energy from the Sun.
- Wood was probably the earliest fuel used by people. Then came peat and coal.
- Peat is decayed moss and coal is decayed trees, etc.
- Coal is mined, sometimes from near the surface (open cast) and sometimes from deep underground.
- Peat and coal have to be delivered by lorry or train.
- Gas is a fuel. Originally it was made from coal but now it is drilled for. "Natural gas" is usually found associated with oil fields.
- Gas can reach our homes and factories by pipes.
- Oil is a fuel. It is always drilled for either on land or through the sea bed. Oil is also a raw material used in the manufacture of many different products.
- Oil can be delivered by pipeline or tanker.
- Electricity is a secondary fuel and is produced in power stations where gas, oil, coal or nuclear fuel is burned.
- Electricity reaches our homes through cables/wires.
- Coal, gas and oil will, one day, be used up. However, energy from the Sun, wind and water are renewable.

EXTENSION ACTIVITIES

- How would the children have kept warm long ago?

- What advantages are there in being able to cook food?

- Find out about coal mining, oil drilling, etc.

- Find out how electricity is made.

- What fuels do the children use at home?

- Discuss ways of conserving energy.

EARTH, ATMOSPHERE AND SPACE

BACKGROUND INFORMATION

- The Sun is the ultimate source of all energy.
- Primary fuels are coal, gas, oil, wood and peat.
- Electricity is a secondary fuel because it is made from burning a primary fuel.
- Coal, peat, oil and gas are non-renewable fuels.
- Renewable fuels include wood, wind, water and the Sun.

MATERIALS NEEDED AND SAFETY POINTS

- Warm clothes for dressing up.
- Flint, matches, lighter (if possible).
- Food, wood, peat, coal, oil, perhaps a small container of gas, as example of fuels.
- Posters of power stations, oil rigs, coal mines, etc.

NATIONAL CURRICULUM ASSESSMENT OPPORTUNITIES

Sc 2/ 2a   Sc 4 / 2b
                            3b

CROSS-CURRICULAR AND EVERYDAY LINKS

History: Fuels and raw materials through the ages.

Geography: Where different fuels are found.
                     How different peoples use different fuels.

Mathematics: Data handling: different fuels used at home, eg for heating. Recording and
                     displaying the results.

English: Imaginative writing: life before even wood was used as a fuel.

Art: An energy-conservation poster.

EARTH, ATMOSPHERE AND SPACE

INTRODUCING THE RESOURCE

THEME BOOK

HOW TO USE

What happens?

Anytime, anywhere.
Especially suitable as follow-up (or prelude) to a class trip to the sea-side, woods, park, a church.

To be read by the teacher and discussed with the children before exploring the school buildings and grounds for signs of weathering.

After looking at holiday photos and pictures following a holiday period.

ACTIVITIES AND TEACHER'S BACKGROUND INFORMATION

ACTIVITIES IN THE BOOK

- What happens to paper left outside?

- The decay of leaves and other plant material.

- Look at crushed shells, sand, chalk, etc (if practical).

- Compare new and old wood. Discuss what you can see. What happens?

- Compare a variety of soils (include some peat and compost).

- Look at photographs of different places. Discuss similarities and differences.

- Insects and other minibeasts found in the soil and leaf litter.

- Compost heaps: how are they made and what happens?

- How our homes are affected by the weather.

- The weathering of stone in buildings.

- How the weather changes the landscape.

EXTENSION ACTIVITIES

- Leave paper outside :
  a) partially buried;
  b) torn into shreds and completely buried;
  c) torn into shreds and spread with marmite.
  Discuss your findings.

- Mix some soils together.
  Add some leaves and small pebbles.
  What have you got?
  Discuss your findings. How can you record your work?

- Place water, stones and seashells together in a jar. Screw on the lid. Shake vigorously and watch what happens.

- What happens to old, rotten, weathered wood in water? What happens to new wood in water?

- Design and make a small compost heap in the school grounds. Which rubbish decays quickly/slowly?
  Which animals visit it/live in it ?

- Design and make a wormery.

EARTH, ATMOSPHERE AND SPACE

> **BACKGROUND INFORMATION**
>
> - Over time, weather affects soil. Water runs into cracks in rocks; it can freeze; the rock splits; with the thaw the smaller pieces of rock show up.
> - Erosion alters the land by action of water, Sun and wind.
> - The decay of plant and animal matter makes new soil.
> - Old wood will be more porous than new wood and will be easier to break.
> - A compost heap needs layers of rotting vegetable matter and soil and is better kept in a waterproof container with drainage holes at the bottom of it. Add worms. A compost heap can also be made in a hole in the ground.

MATERIALS NEEDED AND SAFETY POINTS

- Containers for holding soil.
- Labels.
- Different types of soil, eg garden, compost, sand, shells, clay, peat, stony, etc.
- Lenses, microscope.
- Rotten wood, new wood (treated and untreated).
- Pictures, photographs and books showing a variety of landscapes, buildings, churches old and new.

Safety
- Look out for sharp stones and splinters!

NATIONAL CURRICULUM ASSESSMENT OPPORTUNITIES

Sc 1 / 1a	Sc 1 / 3b	Sc 2/ 2a	Sc 3 / 2b
2a	3c	2c	3c
2b	3d	2d	
3a		3b	

CROSS-CURRICULAR AND EVERYDAY LINKS

Geography: Look for signs of weathering on a journey. Examine types of soil. Look at different terrains and compare photographs and pictures.

Technology: Design a wormery, choosing appropriate materials.

Mathematics: Data handling: differences and similarities between soils/rocks, etc. Bar charts/ sets. Mass of rocks. Time lines and scales.

Art and Craft: Collage: choose materials and tools to make a rotting tree. Make an Autumn collage.

Music: Make a tune for water tumbling over pebbles. Can you make the sound of the sea?

History: Changes in the environment over time.

EARTH, ATMOSPHERE AND SPACE

INTRODUCING THE RESOURCE

THEME BOOK	## The Earth, the Moon and the Sun
HOW TO USE	Conceptually a high ability book. Perhaps best used either as a picture book for initiating discussion, or in small doses.

ACTIVITIES AND TEACHER'S BACKGROUND INFORMATION

ACTIVITIES IN THE BOOK

- The "apparent movement" of the Sun across the sky from Sunrise, through the morning, afternoon and finally to Sunset.

- Twilight.

- "New Moon", full Moon.

- The Moon as seen from the Earth and the Earth as seen from the Moon.

- The Earth, Moon and Sun as solid bodies.

- The Solar System.

EXTENSION ACTIVITIES

- Build a model using a ball for the Earth and a torch for the Sun. Rotate the earth on its axis and show how, to a person standing on the Earth, the Sun appears to move across the sky.
- Find out the time of Sunrise and Sunset and when the Sun is "highest" in the sky.
- Plot the apparent movement of the Sun by sticking a circle of card on a window and marking its shadow every hour.
- Draw the phases of the Moon, either through supervised observation or from a book.

BACKGROUND INFORMATION

- The apparent movement of the Sun across the sky is due to the Earth's rotating once every 24 hours. To us standing on the Earth it appears as if the Sun rises in the East, moves across the sky and sets in the West. In fact, the Sun is not moving but the Earth is rotating.
- Pages 2 and 3 have used multiple exposure photgraphs.
- Twilight is usually referred to as that time of the evening when the Sun has set but there is still enough light to see by.
- We see the Moon, not because it gives out light but because it reflects light from the Sun. Because of the relative positions of the Earth, the Moon and the Sun, the shape of what we see of the Moon seems to alter from a full round Moon, through just half, then a narrow crescent to no part visible at all. These are called the phases of the Moon. Strictly speaking a new Moon cannot be seen at all, so on page 6 we have shown the Moon just a day or so after it was a new Moon.
- The purpose of including the Moon from the Earth and the Earth from the Moon is to give a sense of two separate 3D bodies.
- This is further developed with photos from space of the Earth, the Moon and the Sun. The Sun photo has been taken through a special filter in order to show the violent nature of its surface.
- The relative diameter of the planets and the Sun on page 16 are approximately correct and can be used for model building. The planets are shown in the correct order but not distance from the Sun.

EARTH, ATMOSPHERE AND SPACE

- For more detailed model building, the following may be useful.

Body	Diameter (km)	Distance from the Sun (1,000,000 km)	Orbital period
Sun	1 400 000	—	—
Mercury	4 879	57.9	88 days
Venus	12 104	108.2	224.7 days
Earth	12 756	149.6	365.3 days
Mars	6 794	227.9	687.0 days
Jupiter	143 884	778.3	11.9yrs
Saturn	120 536	1 427.0	29.5 yrs
Uranus	50 724	2 869.6	84.0 yrs
Neptune	50 538	4 496.7	164.8 yrs
Pluto	2 445	5 900	247.7 yrs

MATERIALS NEEDED AND SAFETY POINTS

- A range of posters showing NASA photographs of the Earth from orbiting satellites, and lunar exploration.
- Card, scissors and thread for model building.
- Balls and a torch for model building.

Safety
- Never look directly at the Sun.

NATIONAL CURRICULUM ASSESSMENT OPPORTUNITIES

Sc 1 / 1a	Sc 1 / 3a	Sc 4 / 1d
2a	3b	2e
2b	3c	3e
2c	3d	

CROSS-CURRICULAR AND EVERYDAY LINKS

History: Space exploration.

Technology: Model-building.

Geography: Sunrise/Sunset times through the year.

Art: Drawing pictures of the Earth from space.

COMMUNICATIONS

INTRODUCING THE RESOURCE

THEME BOOK

HOW TO USE

Listen!

Anytime, anywhere.
Particularly appropriate as part of a topic on the senses.

ACTIVITIES AND TEACHER'S BACKGROUND INFORMATION

ACTIVITIES IN THE BOOK

- Different animals have different shapes and sizes of ear.

- Different types of noise and ways of making noise using different parts of your body.

- Loud and soft noises.

- The sounds of the weather — what are they like and can you imitate them?

- The sounds made by different animals — can you imitate them?

- Sounds of the immediate environment — at home, in the street and at school.

- The sounds made by different musical instruments.

EXTENSION ACTIVITIES

- Look at the ears of different animals — their size, position and shape. In what ways are they appropriate to the animal's particular needs?

- Have some fun sending messages by playing Chinese Whispers. How accurately is the message conveyed?

- What sounds do you associate with different sorts of weather?

- Experiment with loud and soft noises using different musical instruments? Is it easier to make loud (soft) noises with any particular instrument?

- Consider the problems faced by someone with impaired hearing. What would be particularly difficult or dangerous for them? What sounds would your class most miss if their hearing was impaired?

- Which sounds travel the furthest - high or low, loud or soft?

- Do sounds travel around corners?

- Discuss how sounds can be kept out (sound insulation).

- Children could record some sounds heard in their immediate environment. Do other children in the class recognise the sounds?

BACKGROUND INFORMATION

- We only hear something when the sound reaches our ears.

- Animals which use sounds for hunting have sensitive ears high up on the head which can be turned and focussed onto a sound source. Animals which use sound in a more general way, such as humans, have less sensitive ears which usually lie flat against the side of the head.

- Low frequency sounds can travel a long distance.

- Some animals hear very high sounds, which the human ear is unable to detect.

MATERIALS NEEDED AND SAFETY POINTS

- Tape recorder.
- Variety of musical instruments.

Safety
- Warn children never to make a loud noise near someone's ear, nor to put any foreign body into the ear.

NATIONAL CURRICULUM ASSESSMENT OPPORTUNITIES

Sc 1 / 1a   Sc 4 / 1c (part)
     2a
     2b
     2c
     3a
     3b
     3c

CROSS-CURRICULAR AND EVERYDAY LINKS

Drama: Use mime and sound effects to act out a story.

Geography: Simple map of the journey to school, showing where different sounds are usually heard.

Mathematics: Measuring distances over which sounds can be heard.

COMMUNICATIONS

INTRODUCING THE RESOURCE

THEME BOOK	**Crash, Bang, Wallop, Twang!**
HOW TO USE	Anytime, anywhere.

ACTIVITIES AND TEACHER'S BACKGROUND INFORMATION

ACTIVITIES IN THE BOOK

- Follows a child's eye view and experience of:

  ✓ - percussion instruments

  ✓ - stringed instruments (scraped)

  - sounds of speaking and singing

  ✓ - instruments which are shaken

  ✓ - instruments which are plucked

  ✓ - wind instruments.

- The concept of an echo.

- Musical notation is introduced.

EXTENSION ACTIVITIES

- Have any of the children heard any of the instruments shown in the book, being played?

- Has anyone in the class ever played one of them?

- Make some instruments in each of the categories:
  strikers, pluckers, shakers, scrapers and blowers.

- Experiment with producing echoes (the school hall or other large room is the best place). Try a range of sounds: which sounds produce the best echoes? Do some surfaces produce a better echo than others?

BACKGROUND INFORMATION

- The instruments shown in the book are as follows:
  pp2-3: cymbals, drums, xylophone (wooden and metal), piano, tambourine, triangle, pipes.
  pp4-5: violin, cello, double bass.
  pp8-9: tambourine, maracas, castanets.
  pp10-11: guitar, harp, banjo, ukelele, sitar.
  pp12-13: trombone, recorder, clarinet, oboe, French horn, pipes, flute, bagpipes, piccolo, trumpet, whistle, bottle.
  pp14-15: trumpet, bugle, French horn, cymbals, euphonium, harp, mandoline, steel drum, tambourine, double bass, triangle, piano, saxophone.

- ✓ Sounds are made when something vibrates, eg the string of a violin, the air in a horn, the metal in a triangle. The larger the thing which is vibrating, the lower the note produced. For example, a long string on a double bass produces a lower note than the shorter string of a violin. Similarly, the shorter vibrating air column of a pipe produces a higher note than the longer, and wider, air column in an oboe.

MATERIALS NEEDED AND SAFETY POINTS

- Plastic pots and bottles, beads, beans, rice.
- Tins, string, elastic bands.
- Polythene.
- Simple wooden drumsticks.
- Paper, card and plastic straws.

NATIONAL CURRICULUM ASSESSMENT OPPORTUNITIES

Sc 1 / 1a   Sc 4 / 1c (part)
     2a   3d
     2b
     2c
     3a

CROSS-CURRICULAR AND EVERYDAY LINKS

Art: Advertisement for a musical band's concert.

English: Looking at 'sound' words.
                 Colours associated with sounds and/or feelings.

Music: Favourite instruments; pitch.

COMMUNICATIONS

INTRODUCING THE RESOURCE

THEME BOOK

HOW TO USE

But...Australia is so far away

Anytime, anywhere.
Appropriate to a topic on Information
Technology and electronic means of
communication.
Also suitable as part of a topic on seasons.

ACTIVITIES AND TEACHER'S BACKGROUND INFORMATION

ACTIVITIES IN THE BOOK

- A wide range of devices, used to store and transmit information, is shown. Which ones can children see?

- The information can be stored as text, sound or image.

- The information can be transmitted over short — and very long — distances.

- Some of the devices have been in use for a long time; others are very recent.

- Contact over a long distance can be established relatively easily.

- The amount of information which is stored on an overseas parcel: name and address, including postcode, of the person to whom it is sent; sender's name and address; stamps; Air Mail stickers; customs sticker.

- Australia is "the other side of the world". What are the implications for the time of day? What are the implications for the time of year?

EXTENSION ACTIVITIES

- Use a computer to store information in a database, eg weather records.

- How many ways can the children think of to send a message to someone else, eg to their home from school? to someone in the next town? to someone in another country?

- Practise using the telephone.

- Consider the importance of the postal system, particularly in earlier times. How do postcodes work? Compare the different times taken for a parcel to come by boat or by air from Australia.

- Find — and carry out — as many different ways as possible of recording what someone else says. Discuss some of the advantages and disadvantages of each one.

BACKGROUND INFORMATION

- The means of recording, storing and transmitting information, shown in the book, are as follows: alarm clock, radio, radio-controlled car, barometer, thermostat (on radiator), telephone, print (books, maps, newspapers, labels, calendar, birthday cards, etc), taxi meter and radio, anti-theft camera, cash till, watch, airline booking computer, weighing machine, arrivals / departures boards, camera, signs, radio phone, clock, tannoy, TV and video, post, tape recorder.

- Surface mail to Australia takes about 6 weeks. Air Mail takes about 5 days.

- The East Coast of Australia is in a time zone 10 hours ahead of the UK, ie when it is 8am in the UK, it is 6pm in Eastern Australia.

- The seasons are reversed, ie Summer in the UK is Winter in Australia.

MATERIALS NEEDED AND SAFETY POINTS

- Paper and pencils for note-taking
- As many of the items illustrated in the book as possible.
- Access to a computer for setting up a database.

NATIONAL CURRICULUM ASSESSMENT OPPORTUNITIES

Sc 1 / 1a
      2a
      2b

CROSS-CURRICULAR AND EVERYDAY LINKS

Geography: Time zones. Seasons.
                  How far away is Australia - in terms of distance and in terms of travel time?

History: The first emigrants to Australia.
                  The history of the postal service.

English: Sending messages. Does the way you write/say the message depend on who the message is for?

Art/Craft: Seasons poster.

Mathematics: Data handling.

COMMUNICATIONS

INTRODUCING THE RESOURCE

THEME BOOK

HOW TO USE

A book of great attraction

Given the need for basic magnetic equipment, the book is best used as part of a topic on magnetism.

ACTIVITIES AND TEACHER'S BACKGROUND INFORMATION

ACTIVITIES IN THE BOOK

- The cover shows lines of force surrounding a magnet.
- Children will find magnets made in many different shapes.
- Magnetic compasses can be used to find your way.
- Sorting materials into those which are attracted by magnets and those which are not.
- Making a survey of where magnets are found in everyday things.
- With two magnets, opposite ends attract each other but the same ends repel each other.
- Using magnetic attraction and repulsion in various games and toys.
- Number 4 on page 13 enables children to "see" the magnetic lines of force around a magnet. These were first seen on the cover of the book.
- The use of magnets in a scrap metal yard.

EXTENSION ACTIVITIES

- Make a collection of different magnets.
- Use a compass to find where North is. Use a compass to "navigate" around a course set up outside the school building.
- Compare how strong different magnets are by seeing, for example, how many paper clips each can pick up.
- Wrap up different materials, eg iron, wood, brick etc, and ask the children to use a magnet to find the iron package.
- Use iron filings to look at the different lines of force around various shaped magnets.
- Explore the idea of using magnets to sort rubbish (see also *Professor Rumbold and the great recycling machine*).

BACKGROUND INFORMATION

- Lodestone is a naturally-occurring rock which is magnetic. Primitive compasses can be made using a small piece of lodestone suspended from a light thread.
- A compass needle is a small magnet, one end of which points towards the magnetic North pole of the Earth. The magnetic North pole is not the same as the geographic North Pole. The magnetic pole moves about 6 miles around the geographic pole every year, which is why navigational maps have to be updated every ten years or so.
- The only materials attracted to a magnet contain iron or nickel. So steel, which contains iron, is attracted to a magnet but brass, which is made from copper and zinc, is not attracted. It is important not to let the children think that all "metals" are attracted to magnets.

- Magnets are found in many everyday objects. Some are obvious, as is shown on pages 6-7, but many are less obvious, eg all electric motors need a type of magnet as do most speakers in radios, telephones, etc.
- A magnet has two "ends". These are usually called poles. One end is a North pole and the other a South pole. A North pole of one magnet will attract a South pole of another magnet. But a North pole will repel another North pole and a South pole will repel a South pole.

MATERIALS NEEDED AND SAFETY POINTS

- A range of magnets, including disc-shaped ones, if possible.
- Some simple magnetic compasses.
- An orienteering or route-finding compass, if possible.
- A wide range of everyday materials for the children to sort using magnets.
- Iron filings in pepper pots.
- Card, glue, thread, paper clips, paints, piece of guttering or other shallow water container.

NATIONAL CURRICULUM ASSESSMENT OPPORTUNITIES

Sc 1 / 1a	Sc 2 / 3b	Sc 3 / 1a	Sc 4 / 2a
2a		2a	
2b		3a	
2c		3b	
3a			
3b			
3c			
3d			

CROSS-CURRICULAR AND EVERYDAY LINKS

Geography: Navigation and early exploration. The Earth and its North and South poles.

History: Early explorers.

Art: Patterns using magnets and iron filings.

Games: Orienteering.

Technology: Designing and making toys and games that use magnets.

COMMUNICATIONS

INTRODUCING THE RESOURCE

THEME BOOK — **Party time**

HOW TO USE — Anytime, anywhere.
Particularly appropriate as part of a topic on celebrations.

ACTIVITIES AND TEACHER'S BACKGROUND INFORMATION

ACTIVITIES IN THE BOOK

- Planning a major celebration: what is involved? — planning food and events; making games using electricity; using a computer as word processor and for database; designing posters.

- How far can noise travel? Noise as a form of pollution.

- What is needed to set up an electric circuit? Safety considerations.

- Timing devices; sound as a means of starting a race.

- Use of compasses (magnetism) and maps. Plan a treasure hunt.

- Recording events - still and video cameras, tape recorder; use of colours.

- Naming colours.

- Exploring colours and their effects.

- Light and sound - which travels faster?

EXTENSION ACTIVITIES

- Plan a school party or other celebration — should it be indoors or outdoors (weather implications?)? What events will you have? Who will you invite? Will there be food? etc.

- Which noises are a nuisance?

- Make some party games which use electricity.

- Use a computer to set up a weather or other database.

- Look at coloured objects in different coloured lights.

- Investigate the use of colour to create mood effects — sad, happy, warm, cold, etc.

- Make a timing device which could be used to time a 100 metre race. How long would it need to be able to time? How will you start and stop it?

MATERIALS NEEDED AND SAFETY POINTS

- Batteries, battery holders, buzzers, bulbs, bulb holders, wires - or an electricity kit.
- Access to a computer for word-processing and creating a database.
- Paper, pencils, paints for poster making.
- Compasses.

Safety
- Warn children of the need for safe use of electricity, and fireworks.

NATIONAL CURRICULUM ASSESSMENT OPPORTUNITIES

Sc 1 / 1a   Sc 4 / 1a
     2a   1c
     2b   2a
     2c   2d
     3a   3a
     3b
     3c
     3d

CROSS-CURRICULAR AND EVERYDAY LINKS

Art: Poster-making.
           Painting faces to reflect different moods.
           Making a poster about the safe use of electricity.

IT: Using a computer as word-processor and data base.

English: Wording invitations.
           Using a tape recorder to record the information and any interviews, prepare a short
           report on a local event.

COMMUNICATIONS

INTRODUCING THE RESOURCE

THEME BOOK	**Light and colour**
HOW TO USE	Can be dipped into as appropriate, eg sunny days can lead to investigating shadows. Could be used in its entirety as part of a topic on light and colour.

ACTIVITIES AND TEACHER'S BACKGROUND INFORMATION

ACTIVITIES IN THE BOOK

- We can only see things when there is a source of light. Objects like people and mirrors are not sources of light. The Sun, a torch and other "lights", are sources of light.
- Things can be sorted into those which let light through and those which do not, eg glass windows/plastic blinds.
- The colour of transparent objects, eg stained glass or cooking oil.
- How to make a room dark. Leads to further discussion as to the many sources of light we find at school, at home and in the street.
- How shadows are made.
- Identifying different colours.
- How colour is used in everyday life and as camouflage.
- Mirrors, their variety and how they have different uses.
- Using mirrors to make a kaleidoscope, a periscope and to do mirror writing.
- Light is reflected by a mirror.

EXTENSION ACTIVITIES

- Using a dark room and a very small torch, explore how light leaves the torch, is reflected off objects and enters our eyes. So we see things.
- Discuss the colour of transparent things. Are they the same colour as opaque things?
- How many different sources of light can the children think of?
- Why have we invented so many different sources of light? eg: a torch can be carried; a fluorescent tube does not cast a shadow, so is useful in the kitchen.
- The colours found in different sources of light.
- Making different shadow shapes and using different light sources to create shadows.
- Ways of sorting colours into groups.
- The rainbow (see also *What can you do?*).
- Camouflage.
- A survey of how colours have been used.
- How light is reflected in a mirror using a torch beam.
- Where the image of a person appears to be in a mirror, ie your image always appears to be as far behind a mirror as you are in front.
- Mirror images of objects and how they are reversed.

BACKGROUND INFORMATION

- Many children believe that when they "see" something, light leaves their eyes and travels to what they are looking at. This is not correct. We see something because light leaves a source such as a torch or the Sun, travels to the object and bounces off that object. This "bounced" or reflected light travels to our eyes, which then enables us to "see" the object.

- Materials which let light pass through are transparent and those which do not are opaque. However, lots of materials let some light through and we use many words to describe them, eg frosted (as in glass) or semi-transparent (as in clothing).
- To make a room dark, both external and internal sources of light must be removed.
- Light rays travel in straight lines, which is why you cannot see around corners. So if you put an opaque object in the way of light, it will stop the light, no light will be able to bend around the object and get in behind it. A shadow is formed. A shadow is an absence of light.
- The colours of the rainbow are violet, indigo, blue, green, yellow, orange, red.
- Light is reflected from a plain mirror at the same angle as it hits the mirror.
- The image in a mirror is reversed.

MATERIALS NEEDED AND SAFETY POINTS

- Access to a room or large cupboard which can be darkened.
- A variety of mirrors and/or some mirror foil.
- Torches and coloured filters.
- A variety of transparent, semi-transparent and opaque materials.
- A battery, wire and lamp with holder.
- A candle.
- Coloured glass.
- Some card and scissors to cut out shadow shapes.

Safety
- Never look straight at the Sun.
- Take great care if using candles.

NATIONAL CURRICULUM ASSESSMENT OPPORTUNITIES

Sc 1 / 1a	Sc 3 / 1a	Sc 4 / 1c
2a	2a	2d
2b	3a	3d
2c		
3a		
3d		

CROSS-CURRICULAR AND EVERYDAY LINKS

Art:	Shadows. Colours and colour mixing.
Drama:	Shadow plays. Coloured lights.
English:	The use of colour in the environment and to express feelings, eg red for danger, red for anger.
Technology:	Making things which use mirrors.

COMMUNICATIONS

INTRODUCING THE RESOURCE

THEME BOOK

HOW TO USE

Our electric home

Given the need for basic electrical equipment, the book is best used as part of a topic on electricity.

ACTIVITIES AND TEACHER'S BACKGROUND INFORMATION

ACTIVITIES IN THE BOOK

- There is a large number of everyday objects which need electricity to make them work.
- The unsafe use of mains electricity, in particular: poking things into sockets, too many plugs in one socket, long wires across the floor which people may trip over, frayed wires, broken sockets, unsafe changing of lamps, unguarded electric fires with young children, electrical appliances in the bathroom.
- There are two sources of electricity in common use in our homes, the mains and batteries.
- Mains electricity is "produced" in power stations and reaches our homes via wires. Once in our homes it goes through the mains fuse box and electricity meter. After that, it goes through wires in the floors, walls and ceilings to the sockets and light switches.
- Building simple electrical circuits.
- Complete circuits.
- Use of switches in making a complete circuit.
- Testing electrical insulation and conductors.
- Building a model light and switch and comparing it with a house lamp and switch.
- Building electrical toys, using lights, buzzers, motors etc.
- Unusual or very modern uses of electricity.

EXTENSION ACTIVITIES

- Make a list of the things at home which need electricity to make them work.
- Divide this list into those which work by batteries and those which work from the mains.
- Design and make a poster, showing the DOs and DON'Ts of using electricity safely.
- A survey of lights, switches and sockets to be found in the school or at home.
- Reading an electricity meter.
- Children could design and build their own simple circuits.
- Compare the use of different numbers of batteries with the brightness of the lamp.
- Are all metals electricity conductors?
- Consider why electrical cable is metal inside and plastic outside.
- Insulation and safety.
- Children could design and build their own electric toy or game.

BACKGROUND INFORMATION

- Many children believe that electricity is found in sockets and batteries. It is therefore important to stress the role of the power station, the national grid and buried cables and wires, in bringing

electricity to the sockets in our homes.
- The mains fuse and meter in our homes are the property of the Electricity Board and must not be touched.
- There is no electricity stored in batteries — only special chemicals which produce electricity when needed. These chemicals get used up and we say the battery is flat.
- All metals are electrical conductors (so are some liquids). All plastics are electrical insulators. So electric cable is metal wire inside to carry the electricity, and plastic outside to make it safe to touch. That is why a worn cable is dangerous as you might touch the wire.
- Safety: Switches and fuses must always be in the live wire. Fuses should be the right size for the apparatus. The earth wire is there for safety in the event of an electrical fault.

MATERIALS NEEDED AND SAFETY POINTS

- A torch and a variety of batteries.
- The use of a mains operated appliance such as a hair dryer.
- Battery holders and batteries.
- Lamp holders and lamps.
- Switches and wires.
- A range of everyday materials which can be tested to see if they are electrical conductors or insulators.
- Buzzers and motors.

Safety
- The safety aspects of using mains electricity must be stressed.

NATIONAL CURRICULUM ASSESSMENT OPPORTUNITIES

Sc 1 / 1a	Sc 3 / 1a	Sc 4 / 1a
2a	2a	3a
2b	3a	
2c		
3a		

CROSS-CURRICULAR AND EVERYDAY LINKS

Design: How we use lights and sockets in the home.

Geography: Where power stations may be built.

History: Homes before electricity was in common usage. Which fuels were in use? What advantages does electricity bring?

Art: A poster encouraging the safe use of electricity. A poster encouraging energy conservation.

NOTES

)96

1997